TO BE A FATHER LIKE THE FATHER

To Be a Father Like the Father

Modeling the Fatherly
Attributes of God

Michael E. Phillips

CHRISTIAN PUBLICATIONS
CAMP HILL, PENNSYLVANIA

Christian Publications
3825 Hartzdale Drive, Camp Hill, PA 17011

The mark of ✝ *vibrant faith*

ISBN: 0-87509-475-9
LOC Catalog Card Number: 91-76511
© 1992 by Christian Publications
All rights reserved
Printed in the United States of America

96 5 4 3 2

Cover Photo: © Peter Correz/Tony Stone Worldwide
Cover Design: Step One Design

DEDICATION

Dedicated to my four fathers: John Phillips (known as Jack) who knew I could be a writer; Larry Kronstrom who, along with his wife, my mother, pushed me to be a writer; Vic Retzlaff, who is proud I'm a writer, even though he'll be too busy working on someone's house to read this; and my Heavenly Father who is the object of what I write. Thanks Dads.

Contents

Acknowledgments

I close my eyes every night looking at the most beautiful woman in the world—my eyes get a bigger treat waking up to the same woman. But little did I realize when I married Kathy that she was also a dedicated researcher and diligent proofreader. She is both of these and I owe so much to her for this book coming to light. No one else would have endured the endless yearnings of a would-be author who only had two chapters written. She pushed me and I love her for it. She also gave up hundreds of hours of quality "snuggletime" to watch my love affair with pen and paper. Though the "mistress" is now gone, your patience is valued.

"Kathy" must be the world's most exalted name. My secretary, Kathy, who typed several drafts of this manuscript, deserves two medals; one for her sweet disposition when I changed my mind 3,000 times; two for her advanced degree in deciphering hieroglyphics. You're a faithful friend.

To my kids, John, Andrew, Meaghan and my niece Ruth-Ann, who make life and love fascinating enough to tell others about.

To my mother, Audrey Kronstrom, who corrected my actions when young, and my facts now that I am older. For a long time you were both father and mother. You will be rewarded.

To my brother and sister, David and Judy, who will be annoyed that I wrote these things down first, I thank you for your input all through my life.

To Harry Bolwyn, my would-be business manager. You did more than you'll ever know.

To Paul Gunther, Pete Larson and Brad Rauch for letting me bounce my ideas off of you. And to Carl Naldrett, Linda Hyslip, Don Matheson, Synoia Olson and Hazel Dalke just for saying:

"We know you can do it—get working, Turkey!"

To Jim Berkeley who helped me over the years to hone some of my writing skills. If I made mistakes, it is not your fault, Jim.

To Marge Retzlaff, who wonders why she is included here, but has done more for me than most people in this lazy, yet busy, world.

Thank you all.

Michael E. Phillips
April 1991

Preface

God is called "The Father." When you become a father, you enter the line of work that God has been a part of forever.

This thought fills me with both joy and fear!

God is not a super-charged human being, and we are not midget gods (nor will we ever be). Father-God is perfect in his fatherly attributes. He has always existed as Father to the Eternal Son. We call God our Father because he is our Creator and Sustainer—and because he has taught us to call him by that name. He will never be any less than perfect. Conversely, no man will ever come close to living out any of God's perfections as Father.

But in my heart of hearts, I am bound to try. I must.

Theologians write weighty tomes that usually filter down through the assembly line of college professors, theology students, pastors, congregations and various others thereafter. Child experts (be they psychologists, therapists, busy mothers or any other brave soul) send their advice down different channels, sometimes reaching some of the same people. The dilemma in this information channeling might be like to a football quarterback who is surrounded on all sides. Theologians say one thing, the child experts say it another way and those who respect and read the works of both feel caught in the blitz. Bitter battles have been waged to decide which ground rules are more accurate: biblical truths or practical advice.

As a father and a pastor, I often feel caught between the two. I find myself asking two questions every time I have to be creative in raising my children. First, are there absolute truths which must be adhered to? Second, how can these truths be practiced? There is a cornucopia of good ideas on how to bring those two considerations together. So why this book?

This is where we come back to our consideration of the perfect God. His exemplary activity as our Father must say something to us as desperate dads. He doesn't hang around the Universe waiting for the Judgment Day so he can get back into the action. He has always been at work—and is working to this day! God lives to provide so much for us; why not also an example of how to be a father?

I said that the idea of looking to God to be my example of how to father fills me with joy. From my earliest days when I sought to copy Sandy Koufax's pitching style, I was always looking for role models.

Over the years, a parade of great men (both famous and obscure) guided me through life's quirks and questions. The problem with them all is that even at their best, they are imperfect. Pete Rose bets on baseball, a President must resign for his indiscretions—the list goes on and on. What fills me with joy is that Father-God has never been less than perfect; not even in his father role.

However, there is a dark side, even in my jubilation. God's perfection can weigh heavily, especially when I *often* fall short of the mark. In this context, Pharaoh looms large in my mind. Through his stubborn, sin-filled, hardened outlook, he caused misery to befall his people. But worst of all, his own child died due to his self-centered clutching at straws. As much as I want to distance myself from that despot, I am just as capable of similar crimes, and therefore I am fearful of even looking at God's example.

But I force my head to turn in his direction. His Spirit beckons me with the word "Come." There is grace for failure and help along the way. There can be wisdom and understanding to replace my parental ignorance. There can be laughter where there were only bitter tears of regret. There can also be holy tears where there were only sarcasm and indifference. I look at my Father in heaven and hallowed is His Name. It is worth all my trepidation to look at him.

Jeffrey McClintock, a noted astronomer, recently wrote the following disclaimer concerning the neutron star:

I confess that I have not found it possible to lock onto a clear mental image of a neutron star, even though such an object is composed of well understood particles and has a simple spherical shape and imaginable size.

(Sky and Telescope Magazine)

If an expert on neutron stars cannot even picture one in his mind, how can anyone expect to lock onto Father-God's example of doing anything that He does? It is impossible.

But for the sake of our children, I am to try and focus as clearly on my Heavenly Father as God's Word and common observation will allow. Please join me in this extra-stellar exploration.

Our rally cry is simple: To be a father like *THE FATHER*.

To become a Father is not hard;
To be a Father is, however.
　　　　　　　　　—Wilhelm Busch

Hear the sweet voice of the child
which the night winds repeat as they
　　　roam!
Oh who could resist this most plaintive of
　　　prayers?
Please, father, dear father, come home.
　　　　　　　　　—Henry Clay Work

Chapter 1

Father-Commitments

B lood was pouring from his nose, and inwardly I laughed. It was easy to find humor in the situation when the blood wasn't mine. My 14-year-old opponent cursed profusely under his helmet as I walked away with an airy jaunt—knowing that my key block had both dislodged his helmet and sent our halfback on a 50-yard scoring run. Then I quickly changed my shoe to kick the extra point.

The score was now 64-0! Today, our team had been virtually invincible. My phlegmatic coach was hopping around on the sidelines like a Rose Bowl winner. Of course, this was only a peewee league in Canada, but he, along with the rest of us, was relishing this victory with pride and confidence—we were the best!

In particular, I had ample reason to feel good: I had successfully kicked all nine extra points. And playing left guard, I was one key in our running attack, which that day picked up over 650 yards. We never swerved from our running style, throwing only one pass the entire game. I was also sent in on defense in short yardage situations to beef up the line. But even with these accomplishments, I felt disappointed.

I hadn't seen my dad at the game, and he'd promised to watch me play. I had never performed this hard or this well, and I wanted his accolades, yearned for his approval. I had constantly scanned the stands but had not been able to spot him.

Dad worked some Saturdays as a telephone engineer. Since all our contests were on Saturday mornings, he missed most of them. But he told me he would be here today, even if he had to quit. If we won this game, we would complete the only undefeated season in the history of that league. So, where was he?

In my mind, an imbroglio of emotions was playing: the elation at having played the game of my life; the bone weariness of a hundred crunching blocks; the disappointment and anger at my dad. How could he have broken his promise and missed this contest?

The gun sounded the end of the game and thoroughly deflated what was left of my hope. As I walked toward the dressing room, I kept asking myself why this meant so much to me. It wasn't just his absence; half the guys never had family members attend the games. It wasn't just that he'd missed my stellar performance; it was the stinging pain of knowing that something had become more important that morning to my dad than me.

In the locker room, the anger mounted when I got my jersey caught on a shoulder pad as I was pulling it over my head. Trying to dislodge it, I ripped it across the back. In a rage, I tore off the shoulder pads and threw them in the direction of the locker.

That's when I realized how quiet the room had become.

Everyone else had been enjoying the victory. But not me. My anger stood out like a sore thumb. Our defensive captain, a good friend of mine, ventured a question, "What's wrong, Mike?" All ears were waiting for the answer I couldn't possibly give.

"Tell ya later," I said, hoping to put him off. "It's nothing special." That seemed enough to satisfy the collective curiosity. They all went back to their partying, and I put a lid on my steam. I quickly changed into my old jeans and T-shirt and left the room. I barely acknowledged the congratulations of the coach who commented on my three league records: most converts, longest kick-off and most yardage kick-off total for one game.

I ran down the cement gangway, fighting back tears that confused me as much as they annoyed me. I needed Dad more than I had ever admitted to myself. Walking up the concrete stairs became a chore. But when I reached the outer walkway, I heard a voice call out behind me.

"Wait a minute, superstar—let me buy you lunch!"

It was my dad! He was coming out of the walkway gate. His arms opened wide to embrace me, and I flew to meet him.

"I thought you weren't here, Dad. I looked all over for you."

"I was sitting right behind your bench, down at field level. Didn't you hear me calling out your name?"

Actually, I hadn't heard or seen anything at field level. All my attention had been focused on the grandstand. In a logical, gridlike pattern, I had spent the game scanning the stands. I never thought to look at field level for my dad.

"Quite a passing attack you guys have," my father quipped.

"Yeah, right," I retorted, not letting him go. This was all I ever wanted or needed. He was there as he said he would be.

Commitment

My dad was there for that game, but it wasn't long before he left my life forever. He died one month before my 17th birthday. At the funeral, I couldn't cry. The pain was imbedded so deep, like lava beneath the earth. And it would take four years for the emotion to find a fissure through which to escape. He would no longer be there as he'd promised. He did not live for *my* forever.

I recall reading a major news magazine a few years ago, when the media was replaying the tragedy of the Challenger space shuttle accident. The most disheartening aspect of that scene was the comment made by the son of the flight commander.

The realization of what had happened began to pass over the crowd in a wave of horror. But this small boy stood thinking. As the implications filtered down to the level of his understanding, he began to weep and shudder. Suddenly, he began to call out for his daddy. As his grief mounted he finally cried out with a loud voice, "Daddy, you promised you'd come back—you promised—you said you would!"

His father had broken his commitment to his son, though unintentionally.

Commitment. It is the embryo from which fatherhood must grow to girth and maturity. Fathers and their children form a holy circle whose center point is their commitment to one another. And the strongest force in this circle (inevitably the force that binds it together) is the father's stated, implied and fulfilled promises to his children.

Commitment. It is a heavy word, weighted down with cultural anvils and a thousand reasons for guilt. From one perspective, it looks safe, reminding us that we have purpose in life because of our commitments. From the other side, it is a taskmaster, placing us on the rack when we spend hours playing golf instead of reading *The Berenstain Bears and the Moving Day* for the 65th time that month to our son or daughter.

Commitment. It is slippery in definition, constantly before us, standard as apple pie, felt deeply like spring love and, at times, avoided like the plague.

Fatherhood means being there

My wife, Kathy, and I like to read the "New Arrivals" section of our small-town newspaper. We like to moan in empathy when we read about newborns that weighed 11 pounds. We wonder why Jill and Frank Hack would name their son Zachary. We chuckle as we read about the Crenshaws. At one time, he was the town playboy. Now his wife is giving birth to their fifth child. We comment on how fatherhood has changed this man into a semblance of a responsible adult. He certainly is *responsible*, in more ways than one.

But what constantly disturbs us is that even in our conservative hamlet, almost half the birth announcements list only the name of the mother. There are men everywhere who have shucked their father-commitment like a pea-pod, leaving children who are forced to deal with a huge missing piece in the already tough puzzle of life.

Bobby Kennedy was well known as a senator, an attorney general, a would-be president and as a brother, a son and a victim. But he was also a father. His daughter, Kathleen, eldest of 11 children, remembers her dad as someone who threw maximum effort into his fatherly role. In an interview in the May 1988 issue of *McCalls* magazine, she recalled that:

When he came home from work, all of us

would rush to the door and wrestle him to the ground. . . . The next morning when he left, he never got away without another round of tickle-tumbling, which he endured happily. I guess that's why he always looked so rumpled when he got to the Department of Justice or his senate office!

Bobby Kennedy was a father—a word that is more than a title and more than an obligation. For him, it meant that he was the creator of 11 lives and, therefore, the consummate center of their existence.

As he tumbled and twisted with his creations, there was a renewing of the common life that flowed from him to them. Their energy was the spiritual return on his creative investment. A father breathes life into children and that energy flows back to him with the life it was endowed with.

Bobby Kennedy is a personification of father-commitment. But defining this kind of commitment is not as simple as taking case histories and examining them under a microscope. "For example" does not *teach* us commitment unless that example is God.

God's example of father-commitment shows us that a father is committed when he fulfills four essential elements: *recognition, duration, integration* and *justification*. Each of these gives a father a different handhold as he seeks to hang onto his commitment. Allow me then to use these four parameters to build a working definition of father-commitment.

1. **Recognition.** Father-commitment is the recognition that any children born to a man and his wife are to be acknowledged and accepted as his responsibility.

2. **Duration.** There is no time limit on father-commitment, only a shift in role, degree and approach in fulfillment of the responsibility.

3. **Integration.** Father-commitment is to be viewed as a process that seeks to integrate the freedom of the child with the lordship and guidance of the father.

4. **Justification.** Father-commitment recognizes that God has designed families in such a way that the father is the human initiator and sustainer of all relationships within that family.

The purpose of this chapter is to build a foundation for the rest of the book. Good building practices demand that when you construct an edifice, you dig down to the hardpan—the most solid base available. This will keep what is above from shifting. Father-God exemplifies what father-commitment is. He is our hardpan from which the rest of the book will spring up.

God, our Father in heaven, perfectly embodies all the definitions of commitment that could ever be drawn up. In Acts 17:24–28, Paul preaches to some curious onlookers introducing them to the profound concept of their Creator-God. This scene occurs in the Areopagus, the Greek equivalent of "Meet the Press." Paul's intention is to win their hearts—first to their Creator, then to the Savior, Jesus Christ.

We who are fathers will find in these five verses a gold mine of instruction on the subject of father-commitment. As Paul paints his opulent picture of the superb Father, it is possible to view a tremendous example of how to be properly committed to children.

A recognition of created life

> The God who made the world and everything in it is the Lord of heaven and earth and does not live in temples built by hands. And he is not served by human hands, as if he needed anything, because he himself gives all men life and breath and everything else. (Acts 17:24–25)

A recent news story revealed that an increasing number of young girls (under 16) are giving birth to babies that are addicted to cocaine, alcohol or any number of other drugs. The question that came to my mind was, "Why would someone want to bring a child with those kinds of handicaps into existence?"

After I thought about it a bit, I decided it had to do with selfishness. Many of these teenage girls want company. In their misery and wretched sickness of drug addiction, they want to have a child to relieve the stress of being constantly alone. They do not desire a husband; they want a baby that will give them warmth and a limited amount of relationship responsibilities. Never mind that they later abandon these kids when they grow out of the baby stage.

That same newspaper also carried a story of a man who received the maximum sentence for beating his infant stepdaughter to death. As I read these accounts consecutively, a molotov mixture of shock and anger flew through my mind. Life was not meant to be like this, I fumed.

God, whom we call Father, made this world; He is Lord of it all; He claims it all as His own. He has not separated Himself from us in some other universe. He does not send natural disasters to punish people for the crimes of the few. Paul reminds us that our Father gives life. Unapologetically and irrevocably, He is the acknowledged Lifegiver. To top off this teaching, we must understand that God *planned* to be our Father—it was no mistake.

Two weeks before Kathy and I were to be married, she became sick. My brother jokingly suggested that it had something to do with marrying me.

After thinking about it, Kathy and I decided that the culprit was not husbandophobia (real as that can be) but a nasty little pill she was popping every morning.

Don't mistake my wife for a junkie; she was getting into the swing of nonovulation. In short, she was on "the pill." As a result, her hormones were break-dancing all over her stomach and other body parts looking for ways to make her miserable. In a feeling of near-panic, I asked her if this brand was any better than the last two she had tried. Of course, the answer was no. My wife could not take birth control pills. She still can't.

This left us in a quandary. We didn't want children early in marriage. Yet none of the other methods of birth control appealed to us as much as the simplicity of the pill. We knew we'd have to make up our minds fast; the wedding night was approaching fast.

Several days before the wedding, God and I had a talk, sort of a Father-son conversation—the type my earthly father and I might have had were he alive.

"So God . . . could I get a promise from You?" I started. No answer. I took that as my cue to go on.

"If we don't use any birth control, could You fix it so that Kathy won't get pregnant. I've heard You can turn on the tap—remember Sarah? How about turning off the tap for a year or two."

I waited for God's answer. When He did speak, it was not exactly a voice. He simply steered my mind into His train of thought.

"Why don't you want kids?" He began.

"I can't afford them. Really, God, I'm just getting married. I start at my new church next month. I just graduated from college." On and on my excuses went.

"And you'd love some money in the bank for a change," God interrupted.

"Yes. I knew You'd understand my fears, Father.

Kathy and I don't really want kids now. I don't think I'm ready for the father bit. How about a dog? We'll name him Joshua or something. How about Elijah? You liked him."

Then the conversation took a more serious turn. I could tell by the dark clouds looming over my head.

"Mike, children are a gift I give My loved ones. Do you think I would give you a child if I didn't want you to have one?"

In all fidelity, I can tell you that this last question stayed in my mind for a long time. It stunned me with its logic and candor. It also challenged my sense of devotion and the level of trust I placed in God.

Not the result of a whim

In Acts 17 Paul reminds us that mankind was not the result of a whim. It was a decision that was based on a desire, much like the procreative act of a man and a woman ought to be. Somewhere in the quiescence of time, God exploded with His triune decision: "Let us make man in our image" (Genesis 1:26). And this same God knew every possibility, every probability, every nuance of man's existence. Despite the many negative possibilities, He desired to give birth to our race anyway and to risk everything—even the life of His Son, to maintain that relationship with us.

"That's fine for You, Father," I continually think. "You knew what to expect. I didn't know that when you have two boys and three cookies they both want two. I didn't know you could have an entire dinner conversation about who didn't belch during prayer. No manual on earth could have prepared me for settling arguments about who gets to sit in the front seat of the car when we go to the dump."

Father-commitment for me was begun under a maple tree near my fiancée's childhood home. It was a seemingly benign commitment, not charged with any inner electricity. I simply said, "I'll be Your servant and father to the children You choose to give me."

At that moment two thoughts went through my mind. First, a wave of relief, borne by the Spirit, similar to the feeling we all have when we surrender a valuable aspect of our will to God. Then I remembered a photograph in *Life* magazine: a mother surrounded by 17 sons, with a new baby on her lap. The caption read: "Finally a girl." For some reason, the father had not been included in the photo. Such was my parting thought as I went to tell Kathy that she should stop taking the pill.

She took the news well. After all, she was tired of being sick. When I told her that we could be parents right away if God wanted it, she said, "That's His decision, dear." Then she hurried off to dump the birth control pills down the toilet!

Creation of life through the gentle, passionate bonding of the love embrace is God's plan. The man-who-would-be-father must accept God's hand in the working out of the biblical mandate that says "Be fruitful and increase in number" (Genesis 1:28).

I am not against birth control. We have practiced it many times. But each time we felt compelled to have another child, we agreed with God. And He enabled us—four times! Three were by natural means; one special child was given to us to care for by someone dear. But each child was a separate commitment to make.

I wonder how many fathers-to-be have sat down and considered what they really think about their coming son or daughter. How many view the child as both a gift from God and a mandate to be accepted?

In high school drama class we were drilled on the Stanislavsky method of acting. This method requires an actor to exhaustively study the character he is portraying in order to discover every inner motivation for every action. We should try the same thing in our lives as fathers, for in life we all commit ourselves to actions based on our inner motives.

The motives for bringing a child into this world, at least for a Christian, ought to center on the recognition that God wants to bring about the family—God's great weapon in the war against Satan's tyranny. Our adversary hates cohesion and loves the every-man-for-himself mind-set of today's New Age thinking. Families slap the devil in his anthropomorphic face.

Since God has given us the pattern, fathers should study Him. We begin by acknowledging in our spirits that God wants us to be fathers—in His likeness and style.

Perhaps some time has passed since the birth of your children. Without recognition from you that they are your responsibility, the enemy will bring in the seeds of bitterness, resentment, confusion, anger and frustration when the troubled moments begin.

Recently, I counseled with a woman who remembered forever the words of her father, who said to her when she was a teenager, "I never wanted you." Many fathers have never said those words, but they've lived out their meaning for all to see. It is time to recognize the unique place God gives a father. And the responsibility of seeing who we are and who puts us there.

The duration of a daddy

Oedipus, the famous Greek tragedy, is a story involving two very different fathers. Though the young man Oedipus is best known for his relationship with his mother, it is the tie to his father that holds the crux of the tale.

When Oedipus was born, it was prophesied that he would some day murder his father and marry his mother. In order to avoid these ghastly scenarios, King Laius (Oedipus' father), a superstitious man, sent his son away and made sure the identity of his real parents was kept from him forever. He was adopted by the king and queen of Corinth and raised as their son.

In his early adult life, Oedipus learned of the prophecy concerning his father and mother. Not knowing his real parents, he fled his foster-parents, horrified that he might violate them. On his journey out of Corinth, he met his real father, quarreled with him and put him to death. Then he proceeded to meet the Sphinx—whom he destroyed—and received the Kingdom of Thebes and the hand of his mother in marriage as a reward. They had four children before he learned the awful truth. As his own jury, he put out his eyes and wandered the land in misery.

So much goes wrong when we abandon our children—at any age.

Laius abandoned his child out of fear and a desire for self-preservation. He let him go at a young age and thought nothing of the consequences until his own death. We abhor that line of action; but it is possible that by a different means, many modern fathers are following suit.

How long does God expect us to father our children? Until they are financially independent? Until they leave home? Until they get in trouble? Until we are no longer excited about their "firsts" (first steps, first report cards, first dates)? How long?

Once we become fathers, we remain fathers until the day we die—or until our children do. The Father of all creation sets this example for us in Acts 17:26.

> From one man he made every nation of men, that they should inhabit the whole earth; and he determined the times set for them and the exact places where they should live.

It has been a long time since God snapped His fingers and Adam came together in a dazzling dance of molecular energy. When mankind was young, it needed its Creator-Father and the sagacious training He offers. The Fall of man only magnified his need, for now mankind had an enemy that had not existed before: sin.

What we lacked because we ignored God's revelation, we have tried to make up for in learning through experience, reason and intuition. We are babes in comparison with God, yet middle-aged in our understanding of how our planet does and does not work. But, notwithstanding this, God the Father still cares for us, determining the times as a computer programmer would direct the inner workings of his master program. God still helps us in finding a place to live, in finding our daily bread and even in the wearing of designer sackcloth.

Three fathers

I have had the honor of knowing three fathers (four, if you include the Heavenly One). My first father, the one who begat me and who carried me in his protective arms, shared my life until one month short of my 17th birthday, when cancer claimed his life. My second father, who gave me his daughter in marriage, has become my mentor in a host of life's skills, which include everything from dickering over a new car to decoding the instructions on a can of floor adhesive. My third father, who provided the opportunity for me to be at my mother's second wedding, shares with me his wealth of spiritual insight as he also shares with me a profession—we are both pastors. The two fathers I now have (father-in-law and stepfather to be accurate) still take responsibility for my upbringing. But the scope and breadth of their fathering has different dimensions than that of my biological dad.

My first dad spanked me. I deserved it, believe me. From fingerpainting with axle grease on furniture stored in the basement, to accidentally unplugging the deep-freeze and ruining $300 worth of prime beef, I had ample opportunity to experience discipline. My first dad taught me to laugh and to read, which were his constant loves. He would tell us "shaggy dog stories" that would last for half an hour. He shaped my political views, my moral fiber, my sexual identity. My first dad taught me to love and express affection and to enjoy sports. No one will ever take his place.

But there is plenty of room for the other fathers in my life. In some ways, their roles are of greater importance. In them, I began to see the reason why a father must have active input all the days of a child's life: a father will always be older than his children. My fathers have done things and been places with which I have no experience.

For instance, my father-in-law is an expert carpenter and handyman. Last summer he and I built a porch onto the back of our house. I had never done anything like that. He guided me through it step-by-step, with the patience only an experienced father possesses.

Remember Moses when he was at the height of burnout? He was wearing the judge's robes day and night, and his inner exhaustion was reaching epic proportions. His father-in-law, a man acquainted with giving leadership in his lifetime, gave some timely advice. He helped Moses reorganize his corporate structure and spend more time in training and delegation. Good advice from an old father.

When my four children are older, my level of involvement in their lives must change. So must my approach; no one wants an overly meddlesome parent. But nowhere is there biblical room for deserting my kids when they need me—even when I'm 92 and they're 65. Maybe then I can teach them a trick or two about how to retire gracefully without abandoning my senses and responsibilities. Maybe I can help them be better parents.

Integrating lordship and friendship

March is an uneasy month in the Canadian Rockies. The town we used to live in survives by the local ski hills being full. So we didn't want it to get too warm too fast. But winter's welcome wore thin by March. It is a tough balance emotionally and is hard to bear at times.

This is an adequate picture of the dilemma faced by fathers who desire to live up to their commitments. It is tough to balance the warmth of being a friend with the cold of being in charge. There are definite advantages to both roles, but each one exacts its own peculiar emotional toll.

In verse 27 of Acts 17, Paul explains the reasoning behind Father-God's constant care over His creation: "God did this so that men would seek him and perhaps reach out for him and find him, though he is not far from each one of us."

God points out the path that fatherhood must ultimately take. The responsibility of the care and grooming of our kids is never designed to supplant the personal relationships we ought to build with them. Therefore, the definition of father-commitment must say something about the provider who has time to be the pal.

Father-God yearns to be sought out by His created beings, so much so that He gives mankind every opportunity to find Him. The sending of Jesus His Son had as its ultimate purpose the bringing together of God and His children into a vibrant, moving relationship.

God does not hide, waiting for man to develop the technology and spiritual know-how to come looking for Him. He has made it plain how to have a relationship with Him. And He does everything to accommodate us.

Human fathers ought to be reminded that we do not lose our lordship when we stoop down to offer friendship. Though it may not seem incredibly macho, the man who surrenders himself to the piggyback ride, the "bikeathon father-son crash course" or the "sure my dad will hit pop flies to us" (during hammock hour), will groove into the years of father-commitment smoothly.

Most of the how-to of fatherly friendship will

come later as the parent-child relationship develops. But the why of it all must be believed before it can be achieved.

An older man related a story to me in a counseling session recently that shows what happens when fathers ignore friendship with their children. He was a new believer and had the usual early Christian problems, with one nasty one added in: several months earlier his wife had left him because of his overbearing, critical treatment of her and their five children.

When he became a Christian and began to change, it really bothered him that his family was gone. He made overtures to them, seeking to visit with each of them individually to ask for forgiveness. He especially wanted to reach his twin sons. But they didn't want anything to do with him.

They were young teenagers and extremely protective of their mother. The way their father had denied them his love and, by his own admission, had put their mother on the bottom of his priority list, bothered the twins. When he wanted to take them golfing, they steadfastly refused. They preferred to segue into their new life, leaving him completely out of it.

I suggested he write them each a letter every week, going into detail about his feelings for all his family, remembering cherished family moments and recalling the best times. His answer caught me off guard: "There were no cherished family moments."

In the family album that was his life, he could

not recall one mental image that displayed the family as a vibrant, knit-together whole. He had never made the effort to help his children draw near to him. It was something he had never thought of doing. His own father had stayed away as often as possible during the growing years. He had learned his lesson well.

"All the world's a stage" (according to Shakespeare), but it is the stage God created, upon which the scenes of close relationships between Creator and creation are to be carried out.

A father can lord his position as supplier and maintainer to the point where he does nothing to integrate friendship into the equation. But that is not the way God models father-commitment. Paul told us that God created this world, gives us a place to live and sustains our life, so that someday we will come looking for Him. God doesn't just make planets as a hobby—He made everything so that we would voluntarily join in on the love-bond that He offers.

Father-commitment must stretch beyond recognition and duration and move into the sometimes difficult realm of integration. Children want their fathers to be at their football games, to pay a quarter to watch their juggling act, to meet their new boyfriend (who has a safety pin where a naked earlobe used to be). They want to tell 14,000 "knock-knock" jokes and have you laugh even when they aren't funny. All these seemingly useless things simply tell your children that they matter to you.

A broken main spring

The clock on my wall hangs by two push-pins instead of a nail. As a result, if anyone slams the door, it falls to the floor. Last week it did that and broke the mainspring. And, of course, it no longer works.

But I noticed today, as I glanced at my wristwatch, that the clock on the wall was coincidentally right. The more I thought about that, I realized that even a clock that does nothing is still right twice a day!

The father who makes no commitments to his children will do the right thing once in a while. But full father-commitment means that the father must be willing to move with the flow, bending his will to the constant needs of his children. All the advice and methodology in the world won't budge a father who wants to stay where he is.

Father-commitment is the yearning some dads have that says, "I need help to know what to do next." Only Father-God doesn't need help. The rest of us are bound to garner from Him the strength and wisdom that He supplies. This comes through the revelation of His Word and by His example in the world He created and sustains by His own omnipotent hand.

In the next chapter, we will jump with both feet into a situation we all need God's help with—discipline.

> *Parents deserve reproof when they refuse to benefit their children by severe discipline.*
>
> —Petronius Arbiter

Chapter 2

Spare the Rod and
Spoil the Furniture

W hen we were dating, my wife Kathy and I enjoyed walking the two miles from the Bible college we attended to a local convenience store. Once there, we would share a large soda and romantically sip at it with two straws. Talk of marriage eventually came up during those walks, and it slowly began to dawn on us where this beautiful relationship was headed.

But one afternoon something happened at the store that made us doubt whether we would ever have children. As we were leaving, a boy about six or seven years old quickly pushed past us. As he did so, he bumped into Kathy causing her to spill the drink on her sweater. Just as I was about to say something, the owner came running out the door.

"Hey, boy," he shouted, "hold it right there. What's that in your pocket?"

"Nothing . . . just my hands," the boy answered nervously.

Without another word, the manager reached into the boy's jacket and pulled out several chocolate bars.

"Come with me young man. We're going to phone your father."

"Go ahead," the boy answered with a look of defiance on his face. "My dad won't do nothing. He never does nothing; he don't care."

The boy paused and looked down. After a few minutes, he barely raised his head enough to say to no one in particular, "My dad hates me."

It was a quiet walk home for us. For me, the shock of the boy's admission struck a respondent chord. Perhaps one day I would be a father and have a son like that boy. There was every chance my walking companion would be the child's mother. How would we handle a child like him? Would we be proper disciplinarians? As Kathy and I discussed the matter, we saw a correlation between the father's lack of discipline and the feeling held by his son that his dad did not love him.

Discipline and love

There is a connection between proper discipline and love. And though children cannot always describe the link, they know it exists. As Kathy walked with me, we discussed various methods of discipline we would use when we became parents.

This is an exercise I do in premarital counseling. I give the couple several hypothetical scenarios and ask how they would apply discipline in each situation. Then we talk about God's plan for discipline.

Indeed, the most profound teaching on parental discipline comes from the example Father-God sets. Hebrews 12:10 reminds us that "Our fathers disciplined us for a little while as they thought best; but God disciplines us for our good, that we may share in his holiness." This is a well-balanced axiom that we should learn from at this juncture: Parents do what they think is best—but God *knows* that what He is doing will lead to holiness. In a sobering reflection, we see that He never disciplines awry. Like an expert marksman, He strikes at the bull's-eye of our need.

We are all unique and complex individuals. Perhaps this is why God employed such a quiver of techniques in chastening His children throughout history. Similarly, an array of discipline methods must be employed by parents. These methods help to ensure a measure of exactitude, to gauge levels of growth and to preserve peace in the home.

Not all methods of discipline are to be applied equally. It is often like buying a new car. Each model comes with standard features and a list of available options. As a frugal pastor, I'm usually more interested in the standard features than I am in the options. CD players and leather seats are luxuries beyond my means.

Likewise, in this chapter I will deal with the four most-often-used techniques employed by Father-

God in discipline. The next chapter will explore the optional extras.

Suffering the consequences

Hezekiah is remembered as the king who most resembled his ancestor David. The Word of God describes him as one who "did what was right in the eyes of the LORD, just as his father David had done" (2 Kings 18:3). He defeated the enemy, removed the idols (even the bronze snake of Moses that the Israelites were worshiping) and smashed the Asherah poles. His zeal for the Lord led him to withstand fears from within and threats from without. Among the kings of Judah he was a bulldog of a man, who retained a complete and abiding hope in God.

But Hezekiah transgressed. Second Kings 20 tells us that a man came to Hezekiah with a gift and a get-well greeting from a foreign power. The gift was a diplomatic gesture from Merodach-Baladan, prince of Babylon, who had learned that Hezekiah had been gravely ill.

It is a good feeling to know that people remember us when we are sick. But Hezekiah responded improperly to the gift-bearers' kindnesses. In an effort to impress the visitors with his kingdom's greatness, he showed them all his wealth and accumulated goodies. No doubt these envoys made copious notes of Hezekiah's holdings for future reference (as in "Wouldn't that look great over my mantel?").

Pride was rearing its head in the king's spirit,

and God saw the logical consequence of Hezekiah's pride-filled action. He sent the prophet Isaiah to the king with a distinct message: "All you've shown them will be theirs—soon!"

Here we see one extremely effective method of discipline, one God used many times in straightening out the divided kingdom and its leaders: face up to the consequences of your actions. We see in this account a picture of God who has His hand over Israel when they are seeking Him and calling upon His name. But when they turned away from the Lord, He was not averse to lifting that protection and letting the chips fall where they may.

Why did God use this method of discipline so often? And what makes it so effective?

Perhaps the old radio program, "Amos and Andy" can furnish an explanation. During one episode, Kingfish, giving his view on life, says to Andy, "Good judgment comes from experience." Andy quips back, "Where does experience come from?" "Bad judgment!" Kingfish replies.

Four ways to learn

There are four ways to learn something: intuition, reason, revelation and experience. Children seem allergic to any kind of reason, not terribly interested in intuition and abhorrent of revelation of any kind from any source. That leaves only experience as a teacher.

My daughter's friend recently wore a polka-dot shirt with her jumpsuit to school. The boy behind her, a noted classroom felon, played connect-the-dots on her shirt, using a felt marker. Of course, his antics ruined her shirt.

The girl's parents phoned the boy's parents for a high-level confrontation. What happened next was both mystifying and dumb. Not only did the boy's parents refuse to pay for the shirt, they accused the other family of becoming hysterical. Nothing was ever done to discipline the boy; he never had to face the consequences of his actions.

Two years later, he was caught vandalizing the school. The fact that the parents did not discipline their son no doubt contributed to his delinquent attitude.

Another couple came to see me with an awful dilemma. Their grown son had bought a new car, figuring his new, well-paying job would provide the funds to make the monthly payments. He also bought furniture, stereo equipment and clothes, all charged on his new credit cards. Several months later, he phoned home in tears. He had been laid off, and all his unemployment money was going toward making loan payments. Could they help him buy food and pay his rent?

For four months they gave him money, feeling that their love for this somewhat-less-than-frugal 18-year-old demanded that they get him out of this situation. But they could hardly handle the extra financial load. My suggestion to these caring, helpful people was that they should stop giving him money. I recommended that they tell him to give his car to the bank, take his stereo back to Radio Shack and start living according to his means.

"But we can't do that—he'll hate us," the father exclaimed.

"Perhaps for a while," I said, "but he will never make this mistake again without thinking long and hard about it. After all, God loves us more than any *person*, and He is the strongest advocate of 'suffer the consequences' discipline." They reluctantly agreed with me.

It is difficult to grasp the severity of a situation unless you are the one who must solve the problem. By erasing all of a child's mistakes and baling him out of a thousand sinking ships, *we* learn the value of coping with adversity. *We* learn not to make his mistakes. In short, parents end up learning a lot. The *child* learns nothing.

When I was faced with immediate suspension from college for a serious practical joke, I decided to phone home and get my mother's advice. "I hope they throw the book at you," she said with just enough tenderness to remind me that she really did care. I was floored, however, by her nonchalant attitude. Even after I explained my side of the story, she offered little sympathy. At the least, I had hoped that she would phone the college president and plead for clemency. All she did was wish me well. Though I wasn't asked to leave school, I was disciplined.

I wish I could suggest an age range when this method works best. Obviously, there are some consequences that are too severe (such as endangering a life). And small children do not always see the cause and effect of a problem. But any child who has reached school age is competent to see that when they "accidentally" break the dining room window while hitting a baseball inside the house, their allowance gets diverted back to the "dining room window fund."

Don't desert me now!

Corporal punishment in all its myriad forms still ranks statistically as the discipline of choice among parents today. Though there is more being written in opposition to this form of punishment than in support of it, that doesn't seem to have forced parents to abandon its use.

The word "corporal" has the word "corpse" as its root. In other words, corporal punishment is any punishment that inflicts pain upon a body. God is Spirit, however, and has no hands to spank. But that does not mean that He cannot use physical deterrents.

Consider the children of Israel in the desert— they were a rogue band of rebellious sinners. Whenever things happened that were against their liking, they would have a hankering for garlic, leeks and onions. It was not exactly haute cuisine, but then these renegades were never known for their taste.

The "leeks and onions" crowd were not a deeply spiritual lot, and this continually showed in their lack of commitment. On one notable occasion (found in Exodus 32), the people decided that they were getting tired of two things: waiting for Moses to come down from the mountain and lead them out of the desert and serving a God they couldn't see.

Being the kind of people they were, they came up with a plan to solve both problems. They would elect a new leader and build themselves their own god. They pressured Aaron into helping them in this plan, and the end result was a golden calf. As he presented it to them, he said, with a good deal of irony, "These are your gods, O Israel, who brought you up out of Egypt" (Exodus 32:4). Considering that the idol was a melted-down compilation of their favorite jewelry and gilded spittoons, that statement should have brought them to their senses.

But it didn't.

The order of the day became orgies, drunkenness and general sinfulness as they worshiped the calf-idol. When Moses arrived in camp, "his anger burned" (verse 19), and he took steps to put an end to the rebellion. The final step was killing the perpetrators. He commanded the faithful few to take up swords and go through the encampment putting their friends and neighbors to death (verses 27–28). That day 3,000 people paid for the idiocy of the nation with their lives.

What can we glean from this? Perhaps the most sublime lesson is that physical punishment should be used to ward off destructive behavior. Sin in the camp was to be feared much more than Pharaoh's chariots or a deadly desert. Sin would eat away at the fabric of the covenant relationship as acid searing through cloth until nothing is left but smoke.

God could not allow sin to destroy His people, and so He used the only effective means to discipline them.

Today's culture is no less hazardous than was Moses'. As our children stretch their wings and launch out in exploratory circles, there is a host of dangers awaiting them. We warn them of all we can think of, but when they refuse to heed our counsel, we must reinforce our warnings with corporal punishment.

Young children cannot sense the scope of their actions. Neither are they convinced of the veracity of our warnings. A dad's call to his child not to cross the road without a parent, often elicits, "Why?" "Because it's dangerous" begs the question "why?" again. "Because there are cars!" we finally answer, figuring enough has been said on the subject. But for a child who has never been struck by a car or seen the mess created when this happens, the danger is theoretical. He has it in the back of his mind that crossing the street unaided is not as bad as his dad says.

So he ventures out with quixotic bravado. If the father happens to catch the child, he is left on the horns of a dilemma. The danger is too great for him to constantly reiterate the same warning. If the child cannot sense the pain that would come from being hit by a car, it is time he feels another kind of pain, one that reinforces the warning—a spanking.

The worst and, as far as I can remember, the last spanking I ever received came as a result of my failing to sense my parents' concern over a certain matter. We lived beside a fast-flowing river in which several children drowned every year. I was forbidden to go near its shore.

One day while playing soccer with my brother, I accidentally booted our new ball over the fence and down the embankment. It rolled effortlessly into the river and hovered in a back eddy about two feet from shore. *Surely Mom and Dad would want me to rescue our new ball,* I reasoned to myself. So with my brother's urgings, I quickly retrieved the ball, being careful not to get my feet wet. I was not seen by my parents, and all was safe—or so I thought. What I didn't know was that our next-door neighbor saw me. The news ran the "hot line" to my father, and the rest of the story is noteworthy only to two boys with hot buns. Needless to say, we did not venture near the river for a long, long time.

Reinforce authority

The other reason God used physical punishment in dealing with His children was to reinforce His authority. In fact, the entire wilderness journey was a continual replay of the interplay between God showing His authority and the Israelites trying to exert self-control.

Fathers are given their authority by God, and if children cannot grasp this, then it must be reinforced with pain. Some psychologists suggest that this produces aggressive children, children who use force to exercise their own authority. I do not agree.

Authority is the right to determine what ought to happen. The president of the United States is given the authority to defend the nation. This acts as a safeguard in an evil world. Those in the military who fail to obey that authority are seriously punished.

But there is a difference between authority and authoritarianism. Authoritarianism is the act of applying authority for no reason, and Father-God does not act in this manner. It has no place in corporal discipline. Neither does rage. We must ask God for His patience and loving-kindness.

We should not think, though, that a father should not discipline in anger. Anger in discipline is biblical. God always showed anger when He used corporal punishment. The most effective show of indignation is anger. A child needs to see that we are extremely displeased with his actions. And it will give more credence to the punishment. Spanking a child's rear-end without expressing anger sends him a mixed message.

The key is to use controlled anger. Rage is a loose cannon. We see this in our legal system. A significant amount of time expires between the time when a law-breaker is arrested and the time he actually receives punishment for his actions. By the time punishment is served, the element of revenge is diminished. Justice is served—not anger.

One last comment concerning corporal punishment: I personally believe that the maximum effective age for corporal discipline is about 12. The minimum age is two. After 12, the degree of discipline would have to be too severe to accomplish the right goals.

You're grounded!

Most parents use "grounding" as a means of punishment, but it can be an emotional Pandora's Box. If we view it objectively, though, it can be an effective tool.

When the Challenger space shuttle exploded several years ago, so did the hopes of hundreds of technicians, planners and other assorted personnel in the space program. For two and a half years, the program was put on hold and carefully studied with the intent of trying to pinpoint other problems. Before a space shuttle flew again, *200* changes were implemented. Grounding, in this instance, proved to be highly efficient.

In recent years, there were three separate incidents where passenger aircraft lost parts in midflight. In one case, an engine fell off. Another plane lost part of its roof. And the cargo door and the adjacent cabin ripped off on a third jet. Soon, the FAA ordered all aircraft of similar make and age to be grounded and checked thoroughly.

In an equally momentous decision, I came to the conclusion not long ago that my car needed brake work. Every time I stepped on the pedal, the brakes emitted an ear-piercing squeal. In addition, they were not stopping me with any degree of security. I knew it was time to ground the old buggy. When I pulled the rear brake drums off, I discovered the source of my problem—worn-out brake shoes. What do these examples have in common? Simply put, they followed the same criteria:

1. Recognition of a problem
2. Cessation of activity
3. Discovery of the source of the problem
4. Correction of the problem
5. Beginning the activity again

The Heavenly Father is well acquainted with using this technique of discipline. Human fathers have also seen the value of grounding a child when his actions call for it. But before we consider this method of punishment, we need to answer two questions: When does a child need grounding? What is the purpose of using this technique?

We can learn a lot from observing when and how God utilized this method in His dealings with the Israelites. A prime example of God grounding His people is found in the story of Ai.

As the story unfolds in the book of Joshua, the people of Israel are on a victory roll. If they had been a college basketball team, they would have been ranked number one in the Canaan polls. The conquests started with the resounding defeat of Jericho, and the people in the land feared for their homes and lives. Nearby cities were without hope, knowing that if the nation of Israel could flatten the metropolis of Jericho, their puny villages and towns were buzzard meat. Nothing could stop the Israelites.

Then two things happened that give us a clue as to how God deals out discipline. First, God announced that His children were not living up to the terms of the agreement He had made with them. Second, because of this breach of contract, God was forced to bring Israel's winning season to a premature end. In Joshua 7, we read these ominous words: "But the Israelites acted unfaithfully in regard to the devoted things; . . . the LORD's anger burned against Israel" (verse 1).

Israel was acquiring real estate so fast that the people thought they could forget the rules of their relationship with God. Some of their number had stolen things that were supposed to be set apart for God and then lied about it. And God, their loving Father, ground them to a halt. He took the wind out of the conquering sails.

After knocking off Jericho, the citadel of cities, they looked down the road to their next opponent—Ai. This town was relatively insignificant compared to Jericho and other conquests to come. And Israel should have been able to defeat the city easily. In fact, the decision was made to only send up part of the army. But the easy victory turned into a decisive defeat as the men of Ai routed the Israelites.

Joshua's reaction to the setback shows us why God utilized this method of discipline. He exclaims, "Ah, Sovereign LORD, why did you ever bring this people across the Jordan to deliver us into the hands of the Amorites to destroy us?" (verse 7). In other words, this fledgling commander is wondering why God has put the brakes on his great plans and desires. Self-doubt is sinking in, and that sinking feeling is holding up all the future promises.

But that is what God wants—a slowdown in order for Joshua to evaluate the situation. The Divine Father sensed that these dear children of His were picking up too much speed. The ease with which they attacked Jericho lulled at least one man, Achan, into thinking that his covenant with God was a sure thing—a veritable piece of unleavened bread. God had to stop the whole family in order to correct a malignant attitude.

"I can drive!"

The day their sons turn 16 years old causes fathers to clutch the car keys with a maniacal grip. When I turned 16, I confidently told all my friends that after passing my driving test I would give them a ride to school. But on the day of the test, as soon as the driving tester entered the car, I knew I was in trouble. The guy was "a tie and suit," and I didn't relate to ties and suits. I assumed right from the outset that he was out to get me.

As we got out onto the road, though, I began to relax. The first few streets, turns and questions were all a breeze. My boyhood bravado seeped back through the cracks of my initial insecurity. I was going to beat this system—this tie and suit—and work my way into the hearts of all the beautiful girls!

But disaster lurked just ahead, and it wore the guise of the car's carburetor. It was a touchy thing, disliking anyone who demanded too much. If you stepped on the gas pedal too hard, it stalled. Unfortunately, I made that mistake—in the middle of an intersection—and the engine died. Beads of sweat painted my pimply brow, and the driving tester began writing feverishly. At that moment, I heard myself utter the fatal question: "What should I do now?"

He gave me a look that conveyed three things: "You've got to be joking?" "They're never going to believe this one at the doughnut shop" and "Did your parents have any children that lived?" Calmly, he explained how to start the car and proceed through the intersection.

Things then got worse! In my state of panic, I was no longer in control of my hands. The examiner asked me to parallel park. Then he had to grab the steering wheel as I almost sideswiped the car on the side of the road. He graciously suggested we go back to the testing station.

He must have choked when I asked him if I had passed. He simply told me to get in more practice before I tried the test again. In shame, I phoned my parents to tell them I couldn't pick them up after work. When I look back now, I realize that in my haste to be grown up I neglected to take to heart how absolutely serious an event driving must be.

When my father heard my side of the story, he offered no sympathy. What he did offer was his idea of automotive discipline: No driving and no test for at least three months. During that time he would accompany me on practice drives, instructing me on the dangers of the road.

This grounding had several effects on me. I became aware of how unprepared I had been. I also gained respect for how difficult it is to be a good driver. But most of all, I appreciated my father for slowing me down to the speed of common sense. As a result of this, I actually waited for *six* months before taking the test again. This time I didn't notice the suit and tie, nor did I care. I gingerly drove through the paces, thinking of all that might go wrong. I passed without a single demerit, no small thanks to my father's discipline.

However, grounding can lose its effectiveness when it becomes the only answer for everything. And unfortunately, some parents think that it is the only method to use with teens. They employ spanking until puberty sets in and grounding until the child moves out. I call this an "omelette" problem.

A friend of ours recently let us in on a tightly guarded secret. A local egg producer wanted to get rid of hundreds of extra large eggs that wouldn't fit into the cartons. He said we could have them for a fraction of the price that a store would charge. We took six dozen eggs.

The implication of this decision hit me about the same time as cholesterol poisoning set in. To be brief, I may never be able to look at anything yellow again. Eggs have quickly moved from my favorite breakfast food to the scourge of my life. I loathe them.

The same destiny may await the father who employs groundings to the exclusion of all other types of discipline. It produces resentment, hostility and a certain measure of predictability. Since it is almost impossible to predict the actions of a teenager, why should they have the advantage of being able to predict us?

To properly employ grounding, let's go back to the elements of this cycle.

Step 1: *Recognition of the problem.* Tell the child that there is something wrong that needs to be corrected.

Step 2: *Cessation of activity.* If sex is the problem, for example, dating must stop for a while.

Step 3: *Discovery of the source of the problem.* This is best handled with prayer and loving communication.

Step 4: *Correction of the problem.* (We hope.)

Step 5: *Beginning the activity again.* Redeployment of the original activity sometimes has modifications added. The child gets the car keys back after understanding how to correct his attitude problem.

In Israel's case, God called the nation to a public meeting. He singled out Achan as the offender, and the people dealt with his sin. Observe that God had to stop the march into the Promised Land to get at the core of the matter.

One of our children had been having trouble keeping friends. What truly frustrated us was that she was a pleasant person most of the time and had many endearing qualities. How could we help her get over this hurdle? We decided to ask several of her classmates what was going on. The answer we received was unanimous: When she perceived that someone liked her, she sought to dominate that person's life. She also acted in jealousy if a new friend came in to have a place in that best friend's life or if that new friend was friendly to anyone else.

So we established a rule of limits. We explained the situation to our daughter as we understood it and informed her that if she did not give certain friends adequate "breathing space," we would find a way to keep her off the girls' backs—even if it meant grounding her from seeing anyone. The reason? To give those girls a chance to see other friends. We are pleased to report that not only has this worked but that she now agrees that this was a bigger problem than she first admitted.

Grounding can work at almost any age. Remember, though, that it must aim specifically at the root cause of the problem, and it must not become the only thing in our "refrigerator" of discipline ideas. What child would want "omelette" parents?

The isolation move

We often think of discipline as punishment, but this is not always the case. That is why it is necessary to follow closely God's values in the exercise of discipline. We understand from the New Testament that Jesus Christ came into the world to provide a way of escape from judgment and punishment. God's punishment (meaning the act of God that brings retribution for a crime and has no other purpose) is reserved for those who stand opposed to Him—those who have hardened their hearts against Him.

Discipline does contain an element of retribution, but this is always coupled with another element—*correction*. In corporal punishment and suffering the consequences, retribution seems to play a larger role and correction a smaller one. With grounding these two elements seem equal. The fourth method of discipline, isolation, has more to do with correction than with retribution.

At times, isolation can be almost a pleasant thing. A good friend of mine describes a period in his life when isolation was not only corrective, it was monumental. Ed is a pastor and a man that God has used to show love and healing to many people. But because of a church split and a family illness, Ed felt it would be best to leave the ministry for a few years. As the time stretched out longer than his original plans, some of the old hurts grew into bitter memories. Ed found that it was difficult to work with people on projects without finding himself torn up on the inside and full of anger on the outside.

The other elders of the church Ed attended and I found ourselves confronting him on several occasions. Each time he was filled with remorse and vowed never to get involved in pointless arguments again. But every few months, he would cause another ruckus and then go through the agony of regret, repentance and promises to do better.

After one volatile incident, we felt compelled to pray that God would use more drastic means to help Ed change. Several weeks later, he was hired by the Forest Service to do lookout duty. It meant 25-day stretches of isolation. By the end of that summer, Ed was a transformed man.

Later, he told me what God had done in his life on that craggy lookout posting. The first few weeks, the loneliness caused his anger to mount to a raging inferno. Stubbing his toe would bring an outburst. The longer he stayed up there, however, the more he became drawn to talk to God. He began to develop the art of listening to the gentle voice of the Holy Spirit.

There, in the beauty of nature, surrounded by the many urgings of God's Spirit, Ed made an altar of sacrifice. He laid down the hurts and forgave all who had injured him. In that high place, God released him.

The remainder of the summer became a feast for Ed. He tasted the wonders of God's Word and the beauty of renewed fellowship with God. Today, he ministers again as a pastor, and he is full of love, power, a gracious spirit and a tempered tongue. All this had come about because he was able to get alone with God.

Father-God used this approach many times in the Bible to test His servants and to discipline them. He found this necessary so that they could hear His voice.

Moses is one whom God often took to lonely places. After he decided that being a deliverer was much too heady and dangerous a job for him, he took off running for the nearest hiding place. There Moses found a wife and a father-in-law and at least one son. But being the covenant Jew that he was, Moses looked at his lot in life and said, "I have become an alien in a foreign land" (Exodus 2:22). The Hebrew word for alien is *ger*, which means "someone who is without any rights." Moses felt alone in this land where he wasn't born. It was a hard 40-year lesson, where his handiwork was raising sheep and his memories were the only grist for his mill.

When God came to call him, he was no longer headstrong and determined. He had adopted the flavor of his adopted home and was now quite sheepish. He didn't want the job of deliverer. He didn't want prestige and public awareness. He didn't want to lead millions. The isolation had brought a profound humility in his soul. Through this time alone, where he was without rights and dignity, he learned the discipline of the humbled heart.

Others in the Bible like Saul of Tarsus, King David, Elijah, Elisha and Samuel all had their periods of extended isolation. And each emerged from those times with a new sense of calling, a divine purpose and a more humble stature in life. As fathers, we can witness similar results when we carefully apply the discipline of isolation to our children.

My son has an unusual mind; it seems to be able to exist in several different planes at the same time. He can be eating supper, talking about dinosaurs and thinking about going out for a bike ride all at the same time. For some reason these helter-skelter thought processes have given him the ability to grasp most situations quickly—almost too quickly! At school he is working far ahead of his class in most subjects.

The downside of this situation, though, is that he loves to tell everyone else what to do. He memorizes the TV guide in order to be the first to tell me what channel the hockey game is on. He tells his little sister what she wants for breakfast. He tells his mom that she needs to let him go outside. He tells his friends exactly what they ought to do next. Some people might call him a leader. Others might call him a "royal pain."

He also is not an easy child to discipline. We cannot spank him hard enough, for he has an incredibly high pain tolerance. Making him face the consequences of his actions hasn't changed him much, for he proudly bears the brunt of all negative results, holding his chin up like an exultant martyr.

But when we make him stay in his bedroom alone—he is usually penitent and humbled within an hour. After two hours, he will comply with anything we say. He is such a people person that isolating him from relationships hurts him deeply.

His sense of personal pride often causes him much anxiety. So for his benefit, we find reasons to let him be on his own for a while. The results are always dramatic.

Isolation works best when a parent has to battle pride, belligerence or uncontrollable emotions. My wife employs this method with all our kids when they throw temper tantrums in the grocery store, for example. Somehow they can't see the logic in not buying 70 different brands of sugar-saturated cereals. When they throw a tantrum, Kathy walks to the next aisle. This method of isolation brings them back to her, chagrined and quieter!

As a father, I like to sit down and reason with my children. But trying to reason with one of my little guys while he or she insists on humming "Jesus Loves Me" with a finger in the ear just doesn't work. Letting the offender spend a few moments in the quiet of his or her bedroom changes the situation dramatically!

As we will see in the next chapter, this method does not always work with teenagers. But by that age there are some other specialized tools that can be used to crack through the walls of pride.

These four general techniques are the standard features of God's panoply of discipline methods. Consequences, corporal discipline, grounding and isolation are mainstays in the parent's arsenal of discipline weapons. In the next chapter, we will observe more specialized techniques that Father-God has used. I call them the optional extras.

It is better to build children than to repair men.

—Larry Tomczak

Follow these three rules for coping with your child's behavior:
1. *Roll with the punches!*
2. *Roll with the punches!*
3. *Roll with the punches!*

—Fitzhugh Dodson

Chapter 3

The Optional Extras

I knew what the guest on the radio program meant. What he intended to imply was that some parents are only parents in the sense that they have given a genetic chunk of themselves to their offspring. That's what he meant to say, but that's not what he said! Here's what came out: "Now let's talk about *generic* parents . . ."

Let's consider, for a moment, generic parents. They used to have 1.6 kids, but they must have found the missing .4 children (who were probably still in bed). Now the average family size is two children. Generic parents are always tired, always confused, always repeating themselves and always, always telling one child not to look at the other child. Generic parents come packaged the same as all the rest, because they are too tired to exercise and stay in shape and too guilty to let it all hang out. Therefore, generic parents look the same, act the same, feel the same and utter the same monosyllabic exasperations.

At some point in the lives of parents, the doldrums set in. We begin muttering old, worn-out cliches we told ourselves we would never say, things our parents said to us—"I'm going to count to five, and you had better . . ." or "You're giving me a headache" or "You just wait until your father gets home!"

We do not wake up in the morning "uncreative." No, the monotony of the same old problems in raising the same children drives us deeper into the shadows of these habitual sayings and habits of discipline. Even the methods that were outlined in the last chapter can become as stale and lifeless as food for goldfish.

God never intended that we collapse into a generic sameness in our parenting skills. Creativity is more than the ability to come up with something fresh and new; it is a sixth sense that tells us when something fresh and creative is needed.

More than a quiet household

Discipline must go beyond conformity. It seeks more than a quiet household, an unharried parent and a clean bedroom. The goals must always be instructive and protective. Fatherly discipline is, at its core, a prophetic ministry. Not all of us, however, understand that the tightness in our shoulders and necks is actually God's yoke upon us.

The Heavenly Father never resorted to a constant repetition of the same method of discipline. He wove His creative hand in and out of His children's lives. In the process, they were never quite sure where their unseen Father would come from with His teachings. Would it be the prophet's mouth, the fire's path, the music's cutting edge or the sword's even sharper edge?

Not knowing what discipline their parents might use keeps children on the edge. And being on the edge helps them to learn more quickly.

How do we as fathers know what is the right discipline? The media gives us a hundred, blaring images of teaching and discipline, from the bloodiness of a Rambo movie to the empty-headed tomfoolery of *American Graffiti*. Psychology offers many theories on discipline. Articles in parenting magazines focus on discipline ideas that worked for the writers. The end result is that we often are fooled into thinking that if something works for someone else, it must be right.

While some of these sources may offer good discipline advice, as Christian fathers we should look to Father-God for the ultimate direction in how we are to discipline our children. He used dynamic explosions of creativity to teach and shape His people, which doesn't mean they always listened. But God takes the responsibility of disciplining His children with a view toward success.

My approach to discipline often has been that of a laboratory scientist, experimenting with different methods to see which one works. Many of these methods proved to be failures, and the result was a mess, leaving me to move from my role as scientist to that of janitor. I grew tired of making these kinds of goofs, and I wanted God to show me something that really worked.

Several months ago, the weight of my "Daddy" title was holding me down so much that I felt as if I was going under for the third and final time. I knelt before God and began to pray, asking Him to come into my children's lives and make a difference. I admitted that I felt as if I had been a failure in the fight to properly discipline them. I had scarred them from my many misguided attempts to teach and say what was right.

After a bit, God spoke to me. "Learn from Me," He said. "I will put My words in your mouth and My ideas in your head. Study Me." As I pondered this, one of my children crept into the room. She had come to say goodnight. The sweet luster of her just-washed face made her glow in the dull light. This was God's cherub to me.

She reached out and hugged me as tightly as she could. Then she said, bubbling over with joy, "I sure love you, Daddy!"

I decided that His message to my heart and His messenger, my daughter, were confirming each other. The following is what God has shown me concerning His more unusual approaches to child discipline.

Multiple-choice punishment
Every father has stood in the "angry stance."

Most of us have developed a particular posture that is meant to instill fear and trembling in our children. I place both hands on the sides of a doorway, leaning into the room my children occupy with my mouth curled inward. Perhaps it doesn't sound menacing to you, but it snaps the synapses quick enough in our house!

It would be hard to imagine God's "angry stance." Jonathan Edwards, in his inimitable sermon "Sinners in the Hands of an Angry God," gives us a picture of God in His anger. He compared mankind's dilemma to that of a spider dangling over a roaring fire suspended by a single, slender thread of a web. People who heard the sermon became so terrified that they clung to the pews and lintels, fearing they might fall into hell's inferno.

The book of Second Samuel in the Old Testament gives us another portrait of an angry God. "Again the anger of the LORD burned against Israel," (24:1). Surprisingly, we are not told what the nation has done this time, and we must surmise the crime from the evidence at hand. The problem arises when we discover that the evidence is somewhat confusing.

Verse 1 tells us that God incited David to take a head count of all the men in Israel and Judah of fighting age. Notice that God spurred on David to do this; though he readily cooperated, it was not David's idea. And, on the basis of David's census-taking, God punished Israel. Without going into the theological battle between God's sovereignty and man's freedom of choice, there appears to be a problem here. It seems as if God is angry at Israel but doesn't have enough reason to bring down the hammer of justice. So He fabricates a crime that will deserve punishment. Confusing? Yes. This is not the whole story, of course, but at face value we are not given many other clues.

David sends Joab out to perform the count. He isn't a great fan of this counting plan, and his response to David is nice and diplomatic but not terribly successful. He basically says, "King, I hope you have everything your heart desires, if only we don't have to do this." The good detective asks, "What does he know that we don't know?"

In verse 10 David responds to the results of Joab's count. Is he ecstatic? Does he stand up and throw a dart at the map and say "I declare war on you"? No. He repents. He sees in this confusing drama a sin that is likely to meet with full retribution. He calls it a "foolish thing."

Now you be the jury. God is angry and tells David to count his fighting force. Joab hates the idea before it is carried out, and David calls it foolish after the reports are in. Still sounds confusing.

A rebellious people

We need a historical perspective to get a handle on the object of God's anger. Previous to this chapter, we read of two civil rebellions in Israel. One of them was led by David's son Absalom; the other was begun by Sheba, son of Bicri. The whole nation (give or take a tribe or two) sought to overthrow its king, and it exalted the name of another whom God had neither anointed nor appointed. There was a rebellious, greed-filled spirit among the people which manifested itself in their penchant for mutiny.

In that rebellious spirit lies the kernel of God's anger. As far as can be determined, God had yet to discipline the nation for its rebellious spirit. Now is the time. The possibility is that David himself was beginning to enter into the national spirit. Nowhere does he reject the idea of counting the possible size of an army. He likes the idea of a new draft board being established. Maybe now everyone will see how powerful a king he is and how well he has weathered the two roguish rebels. Self-exaltation and rebellion are sister-sins, and God seizes the opportunity to discipline the whole country in one fell swoop.

God gave David three punishment choices and asked him to choose one: three years of famine, three months of fleeing from enemies or three days of plague. Not exactly a select field to choose from, but David and the people he represented wanted the freedom of choice. They desired the right to delineate their own future, carve their own destinies, lay out the battle plans for their own conquests. Rebellion mixed in with self-exaltation, stirred with discontent and served over a period of security is a recipe for disaster. Therefore God allowed David to choose another disaster to avert the one that was surely coming.

For fathers, this method of discipline has a sparkling quality to it—we cannot be accused of being deliberately autocratic. This is decidedly a democratic destruction. Henry Ford used to say that you could have your next car in any color you preferred—as long as it was *black*. God takes that offer to its ultimate conclusion: He offers three shades of black.

Decision-making is a painful trial-and-error process. There are not many people who instinctively make mostly right decisions in life. There are almost *no* children who do. We can classify mistakes people make into two categories: mistakes of ignorance and mistakes of ignominy. The second kind is made when rebellion is in charge of a child's decisions.

Choosing my punishment

Once when I was a boy, several of my friends had encouraged me to see if I could throw a rock (or rocks) in front of a car without hitting it. My aim was great, but my timing was off. The rock hit the side window and shattered it into a million pieces. I flew faster than the rock up the back alley. The baby-sitter was on the front porch of our house, and the man in the car was just moments behind me. All I could get out of my mouth to the baby-sitter was this: "A man is chasing me!"

I admit it was a trifle misleading.

The 18-year-old baby-sitter refused to let the man into the house where I had run. By that point, I was hiding in the cubbyhole behind the furnace.

The man got our phone number and called my father later that afternoon. By 6:00 p.m., I was still hiding. My parents called for me, but I wanted them to think I had run away. I would have run away, too, if I could have been assured of escaping the confines of our house without being seen. As I listened to my father's ever-increasing oaths upstairs, I realized that the longer I stayed sequestered, the greater my punishment would be. At approximately 8:00 p.m., I emerged with fear and trepidation and slowly trudged up the stairs to face my doom.

There is no logical point in describing the first few moments of the scene as my dad caught sight of me opening the kitchen door. Suffice it to say that it was unpleasant.

The following days were nothing if not patently consistent. I got up, ate breakfast, went to school, came home, stayed in my room, ate supper, stayed in my room, went to sleep. I fully anticipated several years of this torturous treatment. I did not anticipate what would transpire after the third day (and no, I was not raised from my grave).

"Mike, your mother and I have come to a decision concerning your punishment." You have to imagine my confusion as Dad was announcing this. I thought that the confinement and sullen glances were my punishment. I was definitely not prepared for what they gave me.

"Either you take all of your allowance for the next six months to pay for the man's window, or you do some very dirty jobs for me for one month (and the word *dirty* came out coated with film and muck—I had no doubt of the veracity and ugliness of the jobs), or you lose something of equal value from your belongings." And before I could choose the last, easier-sounding option, he added, "And I get to choose which things you donate!"

So much for getting off easy. I spent hours pondering the impact and implications of each choice. If I had been into lists in those days, I would have filled up volumes with negative reasons for each disciplinary choice. None of them was appealing. All of them would hurt. The cruelest blow to my psyche was that I was the master of my own fate—albeit a fate with no happy ending.

I finally chose the chores, thinking that if I did a great job at those, the "warden" would shorten my sentence. As I remember, he did allow me a few days respite near the end of the month. But the rest was a dogged scrap heap of grueling toil designed to weaken the resolve and resistance of a stubborn, young boy.

As we saw in the case of King David and Israel, Father-God used this method several times, and it was always quite effective. Even as I write this, my wife and I are discussing using this punishment with our stubborn son. It has great possibilities, for in his "youth-ness," he has discovered that he has a strong will, fast legs and great timing. He knows that if he agrees to something until the last minute when we are leaving out the door—then throws a defiant tantrum—that we may acquiesce and allow him his own way.

Family meetings

Progressive revelation is the doctrine that suggests that as the course of history flowed on, God revealed more and more of Himself to His people. From the infant beginnings of Genesis, to the full age and maturity of the heavenly glimpse found in Revelation 22, the revelations given by God move from simple and awesome, to complex and magnificent.

Through the Bible, the teaching about God seemingly grows up before us. Therefore, it should be no surprise that God's methods of discipline treat His later children in a fashion more befitting teenagers than infants. In the early books of the Bible, God usually utilized corporal discipline. He resembles the parent of a toddler who knows that reason and rational discussion will never succeed in loosening the grip a four-year-old has on a Fig Newton.

But in the Gospels we meet Jesus, in whom all the fullness of God is to be found (Colossians 1:19). Here, God walked with His children, conversed with them and corrected them; they saw Him and were always training their eyes upon Him, the Author and Finisher of their faith. So in their understanding of God, they grew up quickly.

Therefore, God refined His methods of discipline, utilizing more sublime means to correct poisonous attitudes. One such way He devised is *The Family Meeting*.

The first example of this is found in Acts 15. Just

as Achan's sin in Joshua's day—if left un-
punished—would have sown destructive seeds of
sin among God's people, the actions of the
Judaizers threatened to tear apart God's Church.

The Judaizers taught that Gentiles who believed
in Jesus needed more than baptism. They needed
to be circumcised.

Ponder the peril of this scene for a moment. The
reason Jesus died was to rescue us from a life lived
according to rules—rules we can never keep. The
Judaizers wanted to reinstitute rules that would
overshadow God's grace. Sure, it was only one rule:
Everyone must be circumcised. But you can bet
every dollar in the bank that if this rule had gone
unchallenged, next year's *Christian Handbook*
would have contained 20 regulations for salvation.

God had to put a stop to it!

Father-God could have caused the Judaizers to
drop dead. It is an effective way to get attention
and to stop wrong attitudes. But for some reason,
He decided to use His executive privilege and call a
family meeting. Look at verses 1–2.

> Some men came down from Judea to Antioch
> and were teaching the brothers: "Unless you
> are circumcised, according to the custom
> taught by Moses, you cannot be saved." This
> brought Paul and Barnabas into sharp dispute
> and debate with them. So Paul and Barnabas
> were appointed, along with some other
> believers, to go up to Jerusalem to see the
> apostles and elders about this question.

The Church was growing, and its adolescent ignorance led it into unknown territory. It was obvious to some of the believers in Antioch that an
injustice was being foisted upon them. To others,
this new "requirement" for salvation seemed both
just and justified. If God had sovereignly and personally intervened with "drop dead" authority, it
would not have solved the conflict. The questions
of "why?" and "how much?" and "who takes com-
munion—purebloods or half-breeds or no-breeds?"
would still be whispered around the old meeting
places.

But through Paul and Barnabas, a family meeting is called. As you read verses 4 through 12, you
will notice that all parties in this conflict have
their say. Peter, who is never known to be the
silent bystander, adds his two cents along with the
rest. We are not given much insight into how a
decision is arrived at—except in verse six: "The
apostles and elders met to discuss this question."

The Greek word used here for "discuss" is *horao*.
It literally means "to look into something, to inves-
tigate or to probe by looking intently." It is a good
"father word." When all the family have had their
say, and all the cards are on the table, let's not
make the silly, democratic assumption that the
decision is left up to the crowd. May it never be so!
If my tribe of midgets thinks that my listening to
the spilling out of their grievance box is going to
let them call the shots, they are misguided.

James (see Acts 12), in verses 13 through 21,
gives the compromise solution. This was not a

capricious, off-the-top-of-the-head answer. James informs us as to its source. "It seemed good to the Holy Spirit and to us not to burden you with anything beyond the following requirements" (verse 28). In other words, they looked to God for help in solving the problem among God's children.

Christians recognize how critical it is for the U.S. Congress to look to God for His providential guidance. Hence, there are prayers offered at the beginning of a session as well as from pulpits and prayer closets dotting the country. Likewise, family leaders should petition God for His decisions in their family meetings.

Judge Phillips

I am not an aficionado of "The People's Court" or of Judge Wapner, the show's patriarch. But I have seen an episode or two. No matter how ridiculous the cases look, there always seems to be a hint of validity to each one. Each combatant is asked to sign a waiver, agreeing to abide by the judge's on-the-air final decision.

This system of justice could work in our house. Recently, I wished I had some of those waiver forms for one of our family meetings. Our two sons were involved in a dispute over baseball cards. It was a sordid affair, and the details are unimportant. But I can tell you that their yelling had gotten louder and louder over a three-day period. Finally, at the limit of parental patience, I jumped up from watching the evening news and grabbed the nearest spanking object I could find—a piece of kindling!

When I got to their room, I found my older son angrily clutching a baseball card (a Dodgers player, I think). The younger boy was crying. Obviously, he had lost the tug-of-war. The baseball card had been torn in the fracas and now was basically worthless.

"I have had enough," I said, wielding my big stick. I then announced that I was confiscating all the baseball cards and would hold them until further notice.

Both immediately started wailing, the younger one even louder than he had before. Whereupon, I added a grounding to the confiscation. When this brought more howls, I threatened to spank one or both of them. The vague warning only seemed to intensify their outrage and my indignation.

At this point, my wife intervened and asked me to join her in our bedroom.

"Mike, is this getting anywhere?" she asked. "Can you possibly think that piling on punishment is sobering them? They are too young to understand your anger. Why don't we call a family meeting to get to the bottom of this?"

Some enlightening facts came out of the meeting. We each took turns, stating the facts as we saw them. The rule is that one person (parents included) cannot interrupt another person while he is talking. One son claimed that he was the constant victim of pilfering. He noted several good players who were missing from his collection. The other son claimed partial ignorance, while admitting that somehow one or two truant cards were now in his pile. Kathy had her say—and it was enlightening. She complained about the constant mess caused by 1,000 cards lying on the floor. Little sister had nothing to say, but she did remain dutifully pleasant. I told of my long, working days and my desire for peace and quiet. I confessed to letting this fantasy control me when I doled out punishment. I asked for forgiveness, and they gave it to me.

Then I sat alone for a while to decide an end to the Great Baseball Card Wars. Here's what I decided: My sons should put their cards in storage boxes. Any cards seen lying outside the box after *one* warning would be given to some other young boy in the church. Seven days of clean floors and no fighting earned a free pack of cards.

Each person felt the decision was fair. And so far, it has worked wonders, though there have been a few cards given away.

This method, the family meeting, is needed most when the real issues and problems are not obvious. Unlike the Heavenly Father, an earthly father must recognize that he must bear some burden of guilt. But when all is said and done, the goal of a family meeting is to arrive at a just and equitable solution that is binding upon all parties involved.

The father's chief role is to be the final arbitrator. With God's help, there can be equitable solutions to vexing scraps. Take the time to hear and be heard.

The open wound

It becomes more and more obvious as we study the methods of discipline God used that all His movements evidence a flowing action of grace and mercy. He does not hand out endless edicts, then follow them with minute tortures when we do not follow His decrees. As we analyze the Father's example, one concept is clear: God does not practice punishment apart from teaching. God is always teaching, even though it is sometimes necessary for Him to bring punishment along for our soul's sake.

Sometimes there is great pain in discipline. But the pain comes as a gift from God. It is a marvelous gift; however, we often abhor opening it. (A good book to read on this subject is *Where Is God When It Hurts?* by Philip Yancey with Dr. Paul Brand. Pain is displayed and delineated as a blessing and not a curse, as we are falsely led to believe.)

Once in a while, there is a need for a type of discipline that, while seeking to mend, must also keep opening the wound. God exemplified this approach in the life of His Son. The object of that discipline was the apostle Peter.

On the eve of Jesus' passion, Peter poured out his devotion in effusive emotion. "Even if I have to die with you, I will never disown you" (Mark 14:31).

Promises, promises. If we as parents had a quarter for every grand and noble promise our children made, we could help Donald Trump out of his recent crisis. Promises make good hiding places for the misguided intentions that lurk within us. Peter did not fear pain—he feared rejection. However, to cover up what he should have seen, he uttered his bold bravado.

The truth of his life came out later when he denied Jesus:

> The Lord turned and looked straight at Peter. Then Peter remembered the word the Lord had spoken to him: "Before the rooster crows today, you will disown me three times." And he went outside and wept bitterly. (Luke 22:61–62)

He did deny Jesus three times. And then he was blasted away by the look in Jesus' eyes. Can you imagine the horror of having to look into the eyes of Almighty God the moment you commit the most grievous sin of your life?

I cannot. Its pain is incurable—unless He cures it.

But Peter's life went on. Jesus died, was buried and was resurrected from the grave. He appeared to many people, including the 12 disciples. These turbulent and remarkable events must have whirled past the guilty Peter as war headlines—each truth dramatic, each hooked with the barbs of his own guilt. And so we read in John 21 that Peter retreats from the guilt into the security of the past. He marks that passing with three words: "I'm going fishing."

Children fail. They are our offspring, and we

know how readily we fail. Let us not ever assume that they escape the feelings of guilt and pain because of their moral lapses. The enemy of our souls is not called the Accuser for no reason. He accuses our children continuously, rubbing poison into their wounded consciences, causing them to fester. They may become bitter, guilty and fearful of living life properly. As a lesson for us, we must look at how Jesus, the Father's representative, handles His guilty child Peter.

As the disciples were fishing, a strangely reminiscent scene unfolds. The disciples were fishing, but they caught nothing. Then they hear a voice from the shore telling them to cast the net on the other side of the boat—a scant distance of 20 feet. They do it, and the fish seem to jump into the net. Immediately, Peter and John recognize the man on the shore as Jesus, and Peter, in a fit of emotion, jumps overboard and swims to Him.

Why?

I believe that he saw his chance to be alone with Jesus—finally. We are not told what was said on the shores of Lake Galilee by a forgiving Master and His penitent servant. But we can well imagine. Peter stammered his repentance. Jesus held him in a warm embrace as He forgave everything. Life was permanently restored to Peter.

Then Jesus does what, to many people, would be unthinkable. He brings up the issue of Peter's allegiance. Not once does He do it but three times. Preachers of great repute agree that this triune confession of love is meant to counteract the three-fold denial. That may or may not be true. The most remarkable thing, however, is what is written in verse 17: "Peter was hurt because Jesus asked him the third time, 'Do you love me?' "

Peter was hurt, and it was Jesus who reopened the wound.

Our sin opens a gaping wound in our souls. Into this wound may come infectious emotions, dirt-filled accusations and gangrenous fear and loathing. If a scab forms over these, sealing them in, then the wound must be reopened.

A third-degree burn

Several years ago my wife received third-degree burns. A spoonful of melted shortening was accidentally poured over her hand, creating a coating of heat that burned quickly through the layers of skin. At the hospital the burn was misdiagnosed as a first or second degree burn, and she was improperly treated. The wound became infected when she changed our son's dirty diapers.

When she took our infant son in for a regular checkup, the pediatrician took one look at her hand and ordered her back to the Emergency Room. The infection could send poison further up her arm if it was not treated properly.

After reexamining her, the doctor ordered a procedure that was to become the most painful experience of Kathy's life. She had to return to the hospital every morning and have the wound scraped with an abrasive brush. Then a healing lotion was applied. This procedure continued for 14 days, at which time, it was hoped, the infection would be stopped. It was an excruciatingly painful ordeal, but it worked. Today, she bears no scar from the burn.

There are sins that our children commit for which no punishment would be adequate or applicable. These transgressions may be defiant mischief, rage, spiteful deeds, revenge or injury to others. Scabs form easily over these deliberate decisions to hurt others. As Jesus did with Peter, we must seek to open the wounds and heal them. Sometimes nothing else will work.

One of my boys has a habit that only our family knows about. I am not about to reveal it (for his sake), even though it really only bothers him. He is working on it, and the rest of us have pledged ourselves to silence on the issue. That is, until recently.

My two sons were at the playground with some mutual friends from school. They quarreled over some minor issue and got into a verbal scrap. As the words heated up, the one son revealed his brother's habit to the other kids. They all stood stunned as the realization of what was said sunk in. Partially out of embarrassment, all of the boys went home. Our sons came home in shock. The offended brother had tears flowing silently down his face. The other one was apologizing profusely. It didn't take us long to find out what had happened.

I had no idea how to treat the offender. He had committed a malicious act and deserved a severe punishment. But for the life of me, no punishment came to mind. So I went to my offender son and spoke with him. I explained what was probably going to happen to his brother at school the next day.

The more we discussed the implications of his action, the more horrified he became. He began to cry, and one comment I made brought howls of pain.

I said, "I'm not going to punish you. There is nothing I can do that will correct this." He pleaded with me to spank him or to ground him—anything but what I offered. I made him sit in his sorrow and think about his crime.

Later that evening, he went to his brother and asked forgiveness. They hugged and made up. Then he came to us and expressed his sorrow. We truly forgave him, and he seemed to lighten up at that point. We thought that was the end of it.

But it was not. I continue to see in him the potential for acting in a similar fashion each time he becomes angry. Over the past few months I have watched for anger. When it builds, I remind him of what his wrath did to his brother. This causes him to be hurt, but it also makes him recall a greater hurt inflicted on a loved one.

Perhaps you think this advice is teaching fathers to nag their children. Nagging is essentially a parent's way of saying "I don't trust you." But opening a wound is not nagging. If carefully done, it is a loving way of saying "Don't you ever think of hurting yourself and others that way again." In love, be willing to open the wound.

Contracts and covenants

The last time I caught a cold, it set off a wave of motherly instincts in two women in the congregation. One, a dear friend, came to our door with every herbal remedy known to cure anything resembling a cold. I'm sure the rhinovirus in my nose took a meteoric leap back into the recesses of my sinuses when it saw those concoctions. The other woman brought over her version of a guaranteed cure: the mega-dose vitamin C treatment.

I rank colds somewhere below thumbscrews on my list of favorite torturing devices. Because of this, I dutifully took as many of the pills and herbs as my stomach could handle. Some of the pills were gargantuan, hardly finding space to fit down my throat. And even though I know this was probably not the best medical procedure to follow, I am glad I underwent the ordeal. The next day the cold was gone.

As a result of my bout with a cold and the subsequent healing, I began to think again about God's discipline methods. Taking vitamin C is supposed to prevent colds. Are there forms of discipline God uses to help prevent some misdemeanors from occurring?

The Bible reveals two such spiritual vitamins— and they are much easier to swallow than the cold cures I took. They are called covenants and contracts.

I looked through several of my dictionaries, and

all agreed that these two words mean essentially the same thing. But in the farthest corners of my memory, I recalled a teacher, somewhere, who had made a distinction between the two. Then, in an older dictionary, I found a helpful answer: A covenant is an agreement that says one person will do something if the other meets certain conditions. (Example: I will give you a thousand dollars if you show up on Thursday.) A contract is an agreement that specifies that both people are required to do something for each other. (I will pay you a thousand dollars if you bring me your new Corvette!)

I also learned that the word "covenant" is biblical in origin, whereas the word "contract" is from the foundations of law. Then, as I looked into the Bible, I discovered that God employs both types of agreement. And the purpose of each is to eliminate a need for discipline.

We find a classic example of the biblical contract in Exodus 15. Moses and his brigade of bellyachers had been delivered through the Red Sea and were standing high and dry. Pharaoh and his men were all wet! This miracle by the sea elicited a joyful response from the nation-to-be of Israel. Miriam, the Sandi Patti of that day, lifted up the victor's song on behalf of the people. "Sing to the LORD, / for he is highly exalted. / The horse and its rider / he has hurled into the sea" (Exodus 15:21).

But the people could only party for so long. The long desert road to the Promised Land lay before them, and there was no sense in them waiting around. So off they went with Moses at the helm. Their first stop on this scenic tour of the world's longest beach was a watering hole. It appeared at just the right time—three days after the last water. But this oasis turned out to be a dud, because the water was bad. They named it Marah (which means bitter), more for the way they felt inside than for the taste of the water. They grumbled, complained and shot off nasty little barbs toward the heavens. Did God strike them down for their ingratitude? No, He turned the water sweet.

God wanted to make something perfectly clear to His children—there was to be no grumbling and complaining during the trip. Like one cartoonist said recently, "Columbus never would have discovered America if he'd brought his kids along. Every five miles they'd have asked, 'Aren't we there yet?'" In the same way, Father-God did not want His people complaining every step of the way.

Therefore, he drew up a contract.

> If you listen carefully to the voice of the LORD your God and do what is right in his eyes, if you pay attention to his commands and keep all his decrees, I will not bring on you any of the diseases I brought on the Egyptians, for I am the LORD, who heals you. (Exodus 15:26)

God sounds as if He is a great parent; it is always proper to warn children of the consequences of their actions. And God is always in charge of consequences. He has more means of disciplining us than we could ever imagine. When was the last time you turned the water in the kids' swimming pool to blood? Or turned day into night—I mean we're really talking lights out! Yet in this scene in the desert, he leaves the punishment open to the people's imagination.

An open-ended contract

God drew up a contract that left His part of the deal open-ended. Of course, that was His prerogative. But the genius in a contract with kids is that we spell out exactly what is expected of them.

My children and I drew up an agreement last winter that worked out equitably for us all. I took their final grades for the school year and computed them on a sliding pay scale. I gave them $5.00 for an A and $2.00 for a B. One son was awarded $62.00 and the other $38.00.

There was a rider in the contract that protected against possible failure. If a grade slipped below a C, then a major privilege would be confiscated. The first C meant that one of my sons would lose the privilege to play soccer. The other son would not be able to watch television for a month. Subsequent delinquent marks weighed heavier on the scale. I'm glad to report that I became broke and they kept their privileges. Everyone was happy.

Other parents have told me that contracts work with such things as attitudes, responsibilities, dating life, drugs and alcohol, lying, cheating, pilfering, college attendance and even eating disorders. One notable Christian author advocated the use of a "Teen Contract" with every child when he or she became 13 years old. But before we thank ourselves for being such geniuses, let us remember who wrote the book on contracts—God the Father. He also shows us one thing we may forget: Tough love demands strict adherence to all terms of the contract.

When the Israelites violated the contract, God didn't just say, "I'll forget it this time, but don't let it happen again." He had made an agreement, and He lived up to His part of the deal. God sent plagues and diseases to afflict them. Too many parents shatter the effectiveness of verbal and written contracts by backing out of them when enforcement is necessary. God never did that and neither should we.

So what about covenants? The covenant is a creation of God because He loves to offer grace and loving-kindness. The Hebrew word for loving-kindness in the Old Testament is *chesed*, which probably should be translated, "covenant love." He loves us because He has chosen to love us.

In Numbers 21, we read another account of grumbling by the Jews. They had no specific complaint; the people were whining about this and that. There was no purpose to it, and as a result, God sent poisonous snakes to attack them. God was again fulfilling His part of the contract.

But in this instance, we see God showing His covenant love. He provides a way of escape from the punishment by means of a covenant. He could have eliminated the snakes in a flash. Instead, He ordered Moses to make a bronze snake and place it on a pole. Anyone who looked at it would live despite their snake bites. This was a covenant. God provided the way of blessing. The only decision the people had to make was to look at the snake—or die!

Do you see the beauty of the covenant? The Father promises a great blessing if the children will enter into it. They are not required to live up to an unattainable standard, but rather they are offered a way of escape from the folly of sin.

Forgive me for comparing God to DC Comic's Superman, but the point is more poignant that way. According to tradition, no one asked Superman to protect Metropolis—he just decided to do it. The people of the city could have refused his help, but it would have been foolish for them to do so.

Superdad!

Now to shine the spotlight on Superdad! He is able to leap tall tales at a single glance. He is more powerful than a speeding son who wants to play baseball with his fly open! Yes, it's Covenant Dad!

No matter what our kids do, there should be room for covenant blessings. Blessings are the acts of grace that separate an average father from a special one.

Imagine this scene: It is early Saturday morning. Two boys are sharing a bedroom. One wakes up before the other and decides to get into trouble. He asks his older brother where Mom and Dad store the matches. Big brother smells smoke, but ignores it. It is Saturday morning—time to sleep, even dream. He does nothing to stop the mischief happening in his bedroom, involving some matches, some preschoolers and one pillow.

I was that older brother. The house could have caught on fire if one of my parents had not miraculously awakened. In the grueling ordeal that followed, I was made the scapegoat. At the time, I greatly resented being told I was to blame. I thought my sibling rivals were old enough to reject pyrotechnics as a team sport. Dad told me my punishment was to rake the entire back yard, which was covered with leaves and mushy fruit from our four apple trees.

I toiled for four hours and the yard was still full of leaves. I even cried, more out of desperation than despair. The job could not be done.

I still don't know if Dad saw me crying. But whatever prompted him to do what he did next, I will never forget him for it.

Without a word, he came out and began to rake beside me. He labored, smiling. I don't believe we said two words to each other the next four hours, but his presence inspired me to new determination. When the job was done, he disappeared into the house for a second. Then he emerged with his jacket and mine.

"Come on, Mike. I'm buying you dinner."

Because Dad had driven a taxi, he knew every great eating spot. We went to one of his favorite places, and he regaled me with stories of his teenage life, which evoked both laughter and tears from me.

All along I kept wondering why I was there. I was the guilty felon, not a hero. Yet I was accorded a hero's feast with the king of our household. I don't suppose I could have received a grander blessing from my father. His unilateral action of grace has stirred me to this day not to fail him.

Dad, find as many ways as you can to bless your child—especially when he or she is in the doghouse. Think of the prodigal son returning home, satisfied to eat the stuff they toss into the compost heap. Instead, he got filet mignon. Where is your filet mignon? Do you bless your children with healing and grace? Do you give them a chance to accept mercy when they know they deserve retribution?

No child, young or old, was ever spoiled by a father who lavishes special blessings of word and deed. A spoiled child is the one who always gets what he wants. The child of covenant love is one who keeps getting what he knows he doesn't deserve. Remember it!

The above-mentioned discipline techniques are only a portion of those utilized by God in the Bible. I chose to talk about them because they reflect the two characteristics of God's discipline: teaching and grace. To discipline properly, fathers must communicate.

It's what you listen to when you're grow-ing up that you always come back to.
                                    —Al Cohn

To talk to a child, to fascinate him, is much more difficult than to win an elec-toral victory. But it is also more reward-ing.
                                    —Colette

Speaking Childese—
Fathers and Communication

Parents are capable of communicating well, especially to each other. Ditto for children; they can communicate effectively to others their age. Yet when parents and their children try to speak to one another, it sometimes becomes a messy and even brutal exchange.

I have often wondered why this has to be, and lately, I have come up with a theory. One day my preschool daughter was left at home with me, her sagacious and lazy father, while her mother went shopping. I felt I was entitled to laziness on this Monday, the pastor's perennial day off.

Picture my daughter: braids, beautiful dimples when she smiles, very petite with only 25 pounds of power in her small frame. *I can handle this one,*

I thought as I lounged in front of the television watching a sports program. Little did I realize that my tranquil day was about to be annihilated by my sweet little girl.

Events unfolded innocently enough. "Daddy," she said, batting her eyelashes, "can I have something to eat?"

"What would you like, sweetheart?" I asked, forgetting that parents should never give their children multiple choices.

"I want a bag of M&Ms."

At this point it dawned on me that my daughter had just recently completed lunch and that my wife had said she was to have no treats. I hesitated in my reply, then retreated.

"You've just had lunch, honey," I told her.

"But I'm really hungry," she continued, with a hint of a whimper in her voice.

"You can't be hungry," I said. "You just had lunch."

"Uh, huh. I'm still hungry."

I began to get annoyed, for she was standing between me and the football game I missed yesterday. I tried ignoring her, but it didn't work.

She stood there and whined, "Daddy, I want M&Ms."

At this point, I decided I would try to reason with her. I explained why she shouldn't have any more to eat. I used medical reasons, monetary ones, even spiritual arguments. My debating skills were superb, and the logic was overpowering. But my daughter didn't flinch an inch.

"Now can I have some M&Ms?" she asked after I finished my dialogue.

Then I got angry and attempted to extricate her from in front of the television. She still wouldn't budge and only whined louder. I next resorted to threats. This, too, failed. I contemplated all sorts of ways to distract her attention, offering to read every book on her shelf. I promised her rides and other fun things. She took all this in and concluded: "Daddy, can I have some M&Ms now?"

Any normal child would have seen the many reasons why she couldn't have candy at 1:15 in the afternoon. Any normal child would have been quelled at the threats. Any normal child would have given up trying.

And, as any father, I gave in and gave her the candy. My only command, as I handed over the loot, was that she not tell her mother. She dutifully promised silence.

But, of course, 10 seconds after Kathy got home, my daughter spilled the beans and ruined the other half of my afternoon. I still don't know where I went wrong.

My daughter and I had a translation problem. We could hear every word the other person was saying, but we had not understood what was being communicated. Since communication consists of a shared understanding of concepts and not simply a knowledge of a shared vocabulary, we were literally speaking different dialects. Mine was rhetorical and autocratic. Its verbs were active and imperative, demanding a ready, listening ear. Her verbs were personal and oblique, totally mystifying the weak-willed father-figure.

Father-God knows how this translation problem operates. He once stated, " 'For my thoughts are not your thoughts, / neither are your ways my ways,' / declares the LORD" (Isaiah 55:8). Of course, I am not comparing my communication foibles with God's uniqueness. No matter how far regeneration changes us, our thoughts will never be what His thoughts are. But Father-God takes the responsibility for bridging the communication gap between Himself and His children. And the responsibility for bridging the communication gap between fathers and their children rests on fathers.

Some of the methods that God employed to translate truth to His children have been copied by most of us. But some of them have remained untouched. As with every chapter, the methods that have been chosen for examination are not exhaustive. God will never be finished in His variegated attempts to get His point across to humanity. However, the methods I have chosen to consider are the most common approaches God has utilized.

What they see is what you're saying

Suppose you had a son. And suppose he shirked all of his responsibilities and went out and did one of the worst things he could ever do to disobey you. Then, to top it off, he tried to make it look like someone else did it. When that didn't work, he tried to cover it up. This cover-up fooled few people (but your son who was now miserable, guilty and led to believe by his own twisted logic that he had committed the perfect crime). Yet he could not face you, even though he suspected that you knew all about what he had done.

Is there anything that can bridge the guilt gap and communicate both love and correction to this child? God found a way—with a son named David.

The story recounted above will live in infamy. It is the account of David's adultery with Bathsheba. It is about the murder of Uriah, the innocent husband. This is a triple bill of horrors when we consider that David left the matter alone for many months, even until after the child of the adulterous union had been born. Still, he would not repent.

He had nothing to say to his Father. Wild horses could not drag him from his throne-room to the meeting-place with God. And his throne-room slowly became his spiritual tomb as he was locked in by his sense of having failed God.

In Second Samuel 12 we see Father-God quietly opening the lines of communication. We read:

The LORD sent Nathan to David. When he came to him, he said, "There were two men in a certain town, one rich and the other poor. The rich man had a very large number of sheep and cattle, but the poor man had nothing except one little ewe lamb he had bought. He raised it, and it grew up with him and his children. It shared his food, drank from his cup and even slept in his arms. It was like a daughter to him.

"Now a traveler came to the rich man, but the rich man refrained from taking one of his own sheep or cattle to prepare a meal for the traveler who had come to him. Instead, he took the ewe lamb that belonged to the poor man and prepared it for the one who had come to him." (verses 1–4)

When God chooses a word picture, no one misses the point. Catch hold of the pathos here. The rich man owns many sheep and cattle. The poor man is not only poor, but he has only one lamb, and it is a pet. He and his family feed it and sleep with it. God even has Nathan the prophet call this little lamb a "she."

Above all this, it is David, the shepherd, to whom this picture comes. He no doubt remembered the ewe lambs he tenderly held as he beat off lions and bears.

As he listens to this tale, the blood that had come to run slow due to deception, lies and murder, now runs with a fervor: "David burned with anger against the man" (verse 5).

"The man deserves to die," David proclaims. Probably standing, he becomes a picture of the fearless avenger of right that he had been before. He looked this way and that to see who the perpetrator of the crime might be. God's trap had been set—then it sprung shut.

"You are the man," Nathan said. God has painted a picture worthy of the greatest bard, and the meaning catches David as he brings down the wrath of judgment upon himself. Hoisted upon his own lance, David cannot miss the meaning of this pointed story. When he realizes that his Father has caught him, he says, "I have sinned against the LORD" (verse 13).

Painting a panorama on the canvas of thought

The trouble with children is that they have inherited the capability of being blind, deaf and dumb when it suits their purposes. Like the proverbial three monkeys, they may not understand what we are showing, what we are saying or how we want them to respond.

A word picture is a form of communication that skips the fighting and the confusion when disciplining children. If a parent chooses wisely, the right word picture can send a well-worded message to the far-flung reaches of the most closed minds. A word picture can paint a panorama on the canvas of thought. No matter how impenetrable a child is, he can always understand the meaning of a picture. Here are five things to remember when using a word picture to communicate with your children.

1. *Choose a subject that the child is familiar with*—God chose shepherding, a subject David knew a lot about.

2. *Touch the emotions with the picture*—God has the pet lamb slaughtered. Other emo-

tions such as humor, anger, sadness and fear may also be employed.

3. *Use contributing details*—God added details that reinforced the overall picture. The rich man was very rich; the poor man very poor. The lamb was a pet and part of the family. But be careful not to throw in details that are irrelevant or distracting.

4. *Draw a parallel*—When you choose a story, make sure that it parallels the truth you want to teach. The more you have to stretch the parallel, the less effective the word picture will be.

5. *Give the interpretation*—Without Nathan's bony finger pointing at David and the pronouncement, "You are the man," David would have been searching every pot in the kingdom for ewe lamb hairs. The child must be shown the parallel.

Word pictures are not just for correction and discipline. They also can be useful for teaching spiritual truths. Indeed, the parable is the Father's chosen vessel for simplifying the wonders of the kingdom of heaven.

Over the past five years I have developed a rapport with my kids using a mythical bear family. Each of them has their bear counterpart, which I contort through a maze of images and interesting bedtime stories. Always in my mind is the spiritual mosaic that I'm weaving as they listen to the story. I can honestly say that they rarely grasp where I'm going—even though they know a moral comes at the end of each tale.

Once we spoke about the danger of white lies. Another time we spoke about respecting God and letting Him have the final say in our lives. Other yarns have been about healing, stealing and even male-female relationships. My kids do not tire of these stories (at least they've never told me so), and they have remembered some of the lessons years later.

However, word pictures are also effective when dealing with unpleasant situations. One of our children had a bad habit of putting herself down in front of other people. If the teacher would praise her, she would question the teacher's motives. If we built her up, she would tell us we were lying. This negative attitude was becoming a psychological epidemic. It finally came to the point where all she did was mope and whine.

Schoolwork suffered. Home life was harried. Her siblings became annoyed and refused to take the vitriolic malaise any longer. But no matter how many times my wife and I emphasized our love for her, it was disbelieved, pushed away and rebuffed.

Kathy and I decided we needed to employ a word picture. We sat the child down one afternoon when we knew we wouldn't be interrupted.

The premise we built the story on was simple. Our girl loved to give gifts to people. It was her favorite hobby. Anything lying around, old or new, was grist for the gift-giving mill. We used this as the central focus.

Here's the story: Once, a young girl had some friends that she cared for dearly. As was her custom, she would make beautiful paintings to give to her friends. She loved each one dearly and wanted them to know and receive her love.

One day the girl finally gave the gifts to her friends. They seemed happy to receive them, and they took them home. She was pleased that her gifts of love would hang in the homes of her beloved comrades. Then she set out to visit each of the three to find out how they liked the love-gifts.

The first home had no one inside, so she peeked in the window. She looked around for her painting, but it was not to be found. As she rounded one corner of the house, she spotted it in a trash can, with a great big rip in it. It had obviously been dropped by accident and then discarded as not very important. That friend had no love-gift.

At the second home she was welcomed in. When she asked about the painting, the friend said, "I gave it away." When the girl asked why, the friend said, "I don't believe that I am able to be loved. I gave it to another person I thought you liked better than me."

The girl went sorrowfully to the third house. Here, she was met at the door. "Here is your painting," the friend said. "I cannot believe you love me. No one loves me. I cannot stand to see this painting, which mocks me with your taunting."

As our child sat there, tears came to her eyes. She knew that gifts were signs of love. We explained that we and others had been trying to give her love gifts. The love gifts were discarded, given away and disbelieved.

Within a few weeks we saw an impressive change in our daughter at home. She began to receive love and warmth. It took longer, but the school reports also began to show favorable signs.

Word pictures work because they traverse the canyons of words and hit at the heart of simple communication—a picture!

You can say that again

Since the founding of the United States, legislators have enacted laws to curb deviant and objectionable behavior. Robert Wayne Pelton has recently collected some of these unusual ordinances together into a book titled *Loony Laws . . . That You Never Knew You Were Breaking*. One such law has to do with chickens in Quitman, Georgia. In this town chickens are not allowed to cross the road within city limits. I can imagine some city official swerving to miss poultry on the streets. Becoming angry about it, he enacted a law.

Another loony law is in place in New Orleans, Louisiana. It says that if a person bites someone with his natural teeth, the charge is assault. But if someone bites another person using false teeth, the charge goes up to aggravated assault. You have to assume that this happened more than once in New Orleans to bring such a stiff penalty.

In Hartford, Connecticut, children are forbidden to walk on their hands while crossing a street. One can only imagine that several dastardly felons disrupted traffic with this feat before the patrons of Hartford finally protected the innocent, foot-walking populace.

As laughable as these edicts are, most parents are not above enacting their own loony laws. Most of them are based on the fact that the average father is averse to repeating the same warning or instruction to the same child, in the same way, ad infinitum. For instance, in our house it is illegal to lock bedroom doors unless it is done to protect baby sister. It is equally unlawful to look at someone for too long (as in "He keeps looking at me"). The most heinous crime you can commit in our household relates to our car. Any child who asks more than 10 times, "Are we there yet?" on a trip of less than 50 miles gets sold at the next stop!

Parents hate to repeat themselves. And children hate to have things repeated. So it would seem that repetition is out when it comes to good fatherly communication.

Wrong. Creative redundancy is a biblically approved and quite effective way to convey a valuable piece of information. God often repeated Himself in order to get the point across. Let's explore some examples.

How many times can one person say, "Be strong and courageous" in one lecture? According to God, at least four times. In Joshua 1, the Lord uses that same phrase repeatedly. Was God running out of material? Hardly! In fact, these four "Be strong and courageous" statements form the outline for what God was teaching Joshua.

God speaks the first one (verse 6) as an encouragement for Joshua to be a strong leader. The second time God speaks it (verse 7), He tells Joshua to be steadfast in obeying His law. The third mention (verse 9) reminds Joshua of God's presence. The fourth time (verse 18) the phrase is used, God reaffirms that even civil disobedience will not overcome Joshua. God uses the four repeated statements to build the goals for Joshua's leadership:

1. Be My man who leads;
2. Be a man of God's law;
3. Be a man of worship and prayer;
4. Leave the rest to Me.

Consider also Psalm 136. Every line contains the phrase "His love endures forever." In our congregation we have had the men read the portion that modifies and the women read "His love endures forever." Since the first time we did this, the whole church remembers what is found in Psalm 136.

The name of the fifth book of Moses, Deuteronomy, literally means "The Second Law." God had Moses reiterate the teachings found in the first four books. Not only was this a different generation, this was also a people called to a different world. The old generation had been slaves in Egypt. This new generation was to enter the Promised Land. And beyond repeating the Law, He ordered that every subsequent generation teach the law *continuously* to the next generation (Deuteronomy 6:4–9).

It becomes clear as I study the repetition method of the Father that He uses creative ways to repeat the same thing. In order to show His covenant love for His people, He inspires songs, He uses prophets, He pours out blessings and He lets His people know who gave them the blessings.

Nowhere is God more creatively redundant than in the book of Hosea. Beeri had a son, Hosea. We can only assume that he would have wanted the best for his boy: a good home, a nice wife, maybe a few obedient grandchildren. What Beeri didn't realize is that Father-God was calling the shots in young Hosea's life.

In chapter 1 we read this commandment given by God to Hosea: "Go, take to yourself an adulterous wife and children of unfaithfulness, because the land is guilty of the vilest adultery in departing from the LORD" (verse 2). We're not sure if he married a woman who was morally "loose" or if he chose a woman that God showed him would be unfaithful.

Gomer, his wife, left him and prostituted herself to other men. We are told as we read the book, that Gomer is a picture of Israel and Hosea is a picture of God. God expresses anger toward His "bride" because she has run after other gods, even as Gomer chased after other men.

In order to paint a picture of His love, God has Hosea go to his unfaithful wife. By this time her prostitution has led her into a life of slavery. In

Hosea 3:2 it says, "So I bought her for fifteen shekels of silver and about a homer and a lethek of barley. Then I told her, 'You are to live with me many days; you must not be a prostitute or be intimate with any man, and I will live with you.' "

God's message to Israel is poignant and repetitive: "I love you. I will forgive you. I will come to you and redeem you." The manifold ways and means that God employs indicate that it is necessary for us to keep repeating the important things our children must know—while at the same time, finding different avenues with which to explore the truths.

Where the other communication methods I mention center on God's forthright communication to His children, the idea of repetition shows that the methods should be put together in collective and creative combinations.

"Did you clean your bedroom?"

Kathy and I have long felt that a child's bedroom is his personal castle—that explains the "moat" of dirt floating around it. It also explains why we need a drawbridge to get into it. Has there ever been a child who has repeatedly and effectively cleaned his bedroom without constant repetitive reminders and/or cajoling? If your house is like ours, a regular part of every daily routine is to ask, "Did you clean up your bedroom?" Like David Letterman, I have compiled a list of the Top Ten answers to this question, starting with the least frequent:

10. "Yes."

9. "John messed it up after I cleaned it" (to which the other brother responds and says that it happened the other way around; from this I glean that neither bedroom is clean).

8. "Do I have to?"

7. "Almost" (Ha!).

6. "It wasn't dirty" (Ha, Ha!).

5. "I'll clean it after school" (during the *one minute* I'm not fighting, watching television, eating my snack or doing the report that was due yesterday).

4. "I'm too tired" (unless I can play baseball instead).

3. "It will take too long" (even though they have claimed to have done it in 30 seconds several times).

2. "What will you give me if I clean it?" (no comment).

1. "No" (honesty is always the best policy).

I have often wondered why it takes so long for a child to understand that a clean, neat bedroom is healthier, more aesthetic, easier to get around in, easier to find things in and gets Mom and Dad off your back. But then I realize a few things about a child's bedroom. First, I never cleaned my bedroom, and I turned out semi-OK. Second, the child's bedroom is akin to our storage closet or garage. We clean those only when we have to and stick things into them when they don't belong anywhere else.

Nevertheless, I have decided that repetition will work on bedrooms. About once a month, we change tactics in the communication barrage we call "clean the bedroom." We have alternately reminded, bribed, helped, done it for them, rewarded, punished, inspected, shamed, praised, compared, lectured, used word pictures, made it a game, wrestled while helping, helped while wrestling, fooled and kept charts—all curiously effective for a while. Lately, we have even reached the enviable position of having their bedrooms clean on 50 percent of all days (not to be confused with 50 percent of the time).

If an issue or truth is worth teaching, it is worth teaching again and again. Television advertisers know that if someone is going to buy their products, that person has to be exposed over and over again to the commodity. The school system works the same way: repeat, repeat, repeat. But just in case you think this idea is based on the three networks and the three R's, recall how many times Jesus told His disciples He was going to die and be raised from the dead. Even though they never listened, it did have a marvelous impact when He actually died and rose again.

It takes action

The Civil War is a gold mine of colorful characters and useful illustrations. One such incident points out the value of visual communication.

Col. John T. Wilder, in charge of the Union forces, was presented with the latest and most deadly rifle, the repeater. It had never been used in combat, but its repetitive skills promised a quick victory. But Wilder had his doubts. In peacetime he had been an engineer, not a fighting man. He did not have a head for strategy, only for procedures. He was frantic as he thought about the following day's battle.

Early the next morning, he and two of his adjutants set out in a skiff and crossed the river waving a white flag. Immediately, they were brought to the Confederate leader, Gen. Braxton Bragg. Wilder was a man of integrity, so he told his enemy about the repeater rifle. "Do you think we stand a chance?" he asked.

Bragg was also an honest man. Without a word he ushered Wilder out to the assembled Confederate troops. There they were, at least five times as many bodies as the Union side could boast. Then Bragg showed 18 of the massive cannons that were poised to fire on his brigades.

Col. John T. Wilder surrendered on the spot. Bragg had not spoken a word, but his actions spoke loudly enough.

We have all heard the phrase: "Actions speak louder than words." Never is that more poignantly illustrated than when the actions of Father-God are examined and displayed for all to see.

God's first message to mankind, according to Romans 1:20, was His creation. It categorically displays the "eternal nature and divine power" of our Father. In the words of a modern poet, "God was strutting His stuff." So the first thing God communicates to every man and woman is transmitted without a single syllable being spoken. As we look at the Rocky Mountains, the rocks themselves cry out, "God put this together." From the unseen mystery of gravity to the glory of the sun's perfect rays, God shouts in silence as His trademark actions breathe forth His holy and majestic name.

But God's actions get much more specific and profound than creation. One of these pinnacles of God's lofty truth is spoken in Mark 9:2–6:

> After six days Jesus took Peter, James and John with him and led them up a high mountain, where they were all alone. There he was transfigured before them. His clothes became dazzling white, whiter than anyone in the world could bleach them. And there appeared before them Elijah and Moses, who were talking with Jesus.
>
> Peter said to Jesus, "Rabbi, it is good for us to be here. Let us put up three shelters—one for you, one for Moses and one for Elijah." (He did not know what to say, they were so frightened.)

The original language leaves little doubt as to what occurred. This was a step beyond glorification of Jesus the man. God didn't just cause Jesus to shine; He opened Jesus up so that His preincarnate glory was seeping through the molecules of His human existence. As Kenneth Wuest remarks in his commentary on Mark, "His Godly essence shone through the clay of his earthly body. For a moment, even the barest of moments (for we must remember these were frail, mortal men), Jesus was seen for who He really is: Lord God Almighty!"

So no one would be mistaken about what he meant, Mark used a Greek word to describe the change, *metamorphoo*. It means "to give outer expression to one's inward character." Jesus didn't step behind a rock and come out wearing a white suit that would have been the envy of television evangelists everywhere. Mark states that no one on earth could bleach anything that white! Without a word, He stood before them with the glory streaming from Him as water would burst forth from a busted hydrant. It is no wonder that these men were described as being in "the greatest of fears" (verse 6, my translation).

Except for Moses on the mountain, Isaiah in the prophet's chamber, Daniel in his heavenly vision and John on Patmos, few others have witnessed such a spectacle. We have to ask ourselves this question then: Why did God invest such voltage in these men? What was He trying to say through the "sneak preview" of His Son?

Six days before, Jesus had revealed something to His disciples that caught them off guard. Because Peter had confessed that Jesus was the Messiah, the time was right for further revelation to be given. Jesus unveiled the final objective of His coming: not to usher in political change, but to die on a cross and rise again in order to bring spiritual liberation.

Peter could not fathom this, so he rebuked Jesus. Imagine, confessing that Jesus is the Messiah at one moment and, the next, repudiating His words! Only Satan could inspire such a flip-flop.

On the mountain, God the Father revealed Jesus to His children as the Glorious One. All the words in Jesus' vocabulary had not convinced Peter that He was bound for death. An action was needed to reinforce the words. Once the action was complete, God sent them back to the words of Jesus. The Father's spoken command to the disciples was this: "This is my Son, whom I love. Listen to him!" (verse 7).

The actions reinforced the words and then called for the watchers to be listeners again.

Satisfied PKs

Dads may be fond of lecturing their children, but children must be shown how the lecture is lived before they will believe it. I am presently working on an article about pastors' kids (PKs). In congregations I have pastored, there have been several adult PKs—most of whom were struggling with some form of bitterness for having a father who was a pastor.

My children are not near the age when they will leave home, so I sought the aid and guidance of several pastors whose kids were long gone. I chose these gentlemen because I knew most of their sons and daughters. What struck me about their children is that they seemed generally satisfied and happy about having grown up in a pastor's home. These were not victims, but satisfied customers of the parsonage. What had these successful dads done that others had not? I wrote each, asking them to respond to this question: What did you do to guard your children from events that would contribute to a bitter spirit?

The letters I received back captivated my attention. They were filled with pithy advice and straightforward, man-to-man talk. One man's answer, in particular, emphasized the need for the "show" part of fatherly "show-and-tell." This dad answered from his perspective, and he then asked his children to answer my question. One son replied this way, "Dad, even when I wasn't following the Lord, I knew you and Mom were not hypocrites. When other PKs said that about their parents, I could always say it wasn't true about mine."

Wow! What a testimony of God's grace! I could tell that this answer made an impact on the dad, for he wrote in parentheses below this quote: "Mike, you can't imagine what that statement means to me."

I think I can ascertain what it means—it means that it took a long time for Dad's verbal guidance to sink in. But the lived-out examples never got in the way of the teachings. This man and his wife lived out the character they were trying to communicate to their children. Notice that it was not an antidote for unbelief and spiritual failure. In fact, *there is no vaccination* against rebellion and dissonant behavior. This chapter is about communication, not guaranteed success. That's fiction; this is reality.

Reality says that even if you communicate truth impeccably, some offspring will do the opposite. But if your actions reinforce your words, then when the child screams out for an alternative lifestyle, he won't reject a second look at yours.

Hard to love

Father-God is hard to love. His demands upon us are impossible. When weighed in His balance, we are always found wanting. God is perfect and relentless, a frightening and disheartening combination. I cannot love God because I ought to. You can tell me for five Sundays in a row that I ought to love God, but the fact remains that my obligation to love is hindered by my inability to measure up to His standards.

God can tell me He loves me, but so what? There are times I feel nothing from God—no presence, no peace of mind, no assurance of eternal security. All I feel is guilt. No words can arrest that emotion.

God knows how hard it is to love Him, but He helps us. He *showed* us His love. In First John 4:9 we read, "This is how God showed his love among us: He sent his one and only Son into the world that we might live through him." Romans 5:8 puts it a little differently: "But God demonstrates his own love for us in this: While we were still sinners, Christ died for us." The word "demonstrates" literally means to "set up as an example of something." It's a present tense verb in Greek, which means that it is a continuous activity of God.

Father-God models love, mercy, compassion, integrity, faithfulness, forgiveness, joy, sorrow, power and meekness. For all of these, there are numerous living examples from the Bible. God speaks in propositional truth, spoken through direct communication in various ways. But His actions never nullify a single word He has spoken. Indeed, each act of God reinforces the words and invites the hearer who turned away to come back and hear again.

What to say when they say it right

My sons were three and five years old. They were building some elaborate structure with their Lego blocks in their room while I tried to read in the next room. It was a quiet, rainy Saturday afternoon, and my wife was out. I was left alone with the waifs, and apart from periodic bursts of squabbling, the afternoon had gone smoothly.

I finished my novel and in a moment of satisfaction sat back to eavesdrop on the conversation going on between the would-be engineers in the next room. To my shock *and* delight, they were carrying on the preschool equivalent of a theological discussion. My older son was telling his younger brother how things worked in the world.

"God makes trees and plants them where He wants them. Sometimes people do, but mostly God does," he said.

"But what does He make them out of?" his brother asked.

"Old tree stuff lying around."

"How about rocks?"

"Old rock stuff, I guess," the older brother countered.

"Who gets to tell people what to do?"

"Only God gets to tell people what to do. And they all have to listen!" When I heard that, it sounded like a great summation of childlike obedience to God. I was proud of my son and his granite stand for God. I stood up to go tell him that I was impressed by his proper conclusion. But before I would get there, he added this to the conversation: "And I'm god!"

So much for good theology. What I was hearing, though, was a cassette recording of some of the things I had told them over the years, mixed in with some ideas that just popped into their heads. God had not showed them this; like any children they were playing mix and match with the truth. It is funny when children do it. But it is tragic when adults decide to play God. For the truth to come forth without sticky, cultlike appendages hanging off of it, there must be a planned system of reinforcement when our children finally grasp what we are communicating.

In other words, it is crucial that fathers learn what to say and do when their children say and do the right things.

Consider an Old Testament lesson from young Solomon's life. The greatest desire of his heart was to become a man of God like his father, David. In fact, David had impressed upon Solomon the importance of this by saying,

> So be strong, show yourself a man, and observe what the LORD your God requires: Walk in his ways, and keep his decrees and commands, his laws and requirements, as written in the Law of Moses, so that you may prosper in all you do and wherever you go, and that the LORD may keep his promise to me: "If your descendants watch how they live, and if they walk faithfully before me with all their heart and soul, you will never fail to have a man on the throne of Israel." (1 Kings 2:2–4)

Though Solomon was still young, he carried two massive burdens on his shoulders: the burden of the kingdom and the burden to follow God as his father, David, did. Perhaps these twin weights helped propel Solomon to Gibeon. First Kings 3:4 tells us that "the king went to Gibeon to offer sacrifices, for that was the most important high place, and Solomon offered a thousand burnt offerings on the altar." No one had forced Solomon to do this—and certainly there was no commandment laid upon a new king regarding the vast slaughter of livestock. Something was gnawing at his soul, prompting him to show his devotion in such a demonstrative way.

The omniscient Father approached Solomon that night in a dream and became the wish-granting

Sovereign in a way all of us might yearn for: "Ask for whatever you want me to give you" (verse 5). Had this offer come at a later time in Solomon's life, he may have asked for harems or riches or who knows what—but not this night.

"Give your servant a discerning heart to govern your people and to distinguish between right and wrong" (1 Kings 3:9). Here we see what gnawed at Solomon: He was scared to death of the massive responsibility of leading the nation. The burnt offering was the only means that Solomon could employ to let God know of the tenacious battle in his soul. In the heat of a heart willing to be consecrated to God, all other cares were burned away.

All he really wanted was wisdom.

"The Lord was pleased that Solomon had asked for this" (verse 10). God knew that the young king's heart was seeking the heart of God. He had followed his father's advice and was now seeking to be God's man. Since this was a voluntary act, it brought pleasure to Father-God. As a result, He gave Solomon gifts of unbelievable value: lands, riches, fame and power. These were not so much a reward as a reinforcement of the righteous path Solomon had begun to walk in.

Whether it is an angry shout or a stern look, most fathers have developed a myriad of methods for communicating displeasure. This is not wrong—unless a father forgets to show when he is pleased with his child's actions. The Scriptures remind us over and over again that God is "slow to anger, abounding in love" (Exodus 34:6). He would much rather reinforce the good than punish the evil.

What does God count as good? Again, we can look to the example of Solomon's life: a desire to do things the proper way; a heart that does not look for rewards; and an effort to accomplish the proper thing without being pressured or forced into it. No one told Solomon the answer that would please God; his heart was so fully embracing the task before him that only a selfless request would meet the need of the hour. These three things (proper desire, selfless attitude, voluntary action) ought to be praised and reinforced.

God utilized many ways of showing His good pleasure to His children. Many times He rewarded them. Sometimes He audibly stated His pleasure. At other times, He gave His servants greater ministry opportunities. But in all cases, He let His people know that He appreciated what was happening.

An ice cream reward

My son's Sunday school teacher was in tears one Sunday as I met her in the hallway before the morning service.

"I have to tell you what your son did," she started. I was not looking forward to this, but I was about to get a big jolt.

"We were talking about divine healing today. John told us how he had arthritis when he was a baby. He also told us that God used the arthritis to show His will to you and Kathy. Then he went on to share how God eventually healed his knee. When he finished, several of the other children shared their testimonies of healing as well."

When I heard this, I, too, began to cry. I brushed the tears aside as I prepared to enter the sanctuary. But even as I tried to concentrate on the service, I could only think of what my son had shared, and how he had taken all we had told him and shared it in a selfless, loving way.

When we got home, I made up my mind to show my pleasure to him. After lunch, I asked if he wanted to go for a drive with me. We went down to the ice cream store, and I let him order anything he wanted. Then I told him how pleased I was with him for sharing the healing story in his Sunday school class. After we were done with our ice cream, I decided to share more of the details concerning his healing that he didn't know.

He was fascinated by it all. The ebb and flow of our family life connected with his experience, and he felt more a part of a divine plan. Before we left, we prayed together. I felt a bond begin to form that has continued to this day.

It therefore was not a surprise when two weeks later, he gave his life over to Jesus in a full surrender of his will!

HOW TO LAUGH HYSTERICALLY:
Call up a Stranger. Tell him you work for the Telephone Company. You are working on the line. If he answers the telephone in the next ten minutes you'll electrocute him. Call back and let the phone ring and ring and ring until he finally answers. Scream!

—Della Ephron quoting
an anonymous childlike person

Chapter 5

When Freedoms Conflict— Fathers and Responsibility Training

K eeping up with the Joneses doesn't just strike green-eyed suburbanites; nations, too, are irresistibly drawn to competing with other nations. Never was this more amply and sadly illustrated than in the country of Nigeria.

Though the people of Nigeria gained independence from Britain in 1960, by the early 1970s they were still feeling the need to emphasize their identity as a nation. In 1974 the government developed the "Third National Nigerian Development Plan," which was intended to transform Nigeria from a backward country to a leading, modern-age society.

The plan called for a mass construction of buildings, roads and structures that, by their nature, would transform the countryside. The various construction projects called for 20 million tons of cement! The officials contracted bevies of freighters from around the world to bring in the premixed concrete (estimated to be one-third of the world's supply at that time) to the docks in Lagos, the capital city.

It was a grand, noble and seemingly responsible plan—but it was doomed for failure. Once the cement arrived, it was discovered that workers could only off-load 2,000 tons per day. At this rate, it would take 28 years to unload all the cement! We can all guess what happened to the cement—it hardened in the holds of the ships.

Young nations are usually less burdened by centuries of tradition and bureaucracy than are nations that have existed for years. But with the tradition and bureaucracy of older countries comes experience—something that would have helped the Nigerian government see the "holes" in its grand plan.

Children could be compared to new nations: They are headstrong and idealistic, impressionable and impulsive. And these are not characteristics that create responsible attitudes and actions. We could say that children are inherently irresponsible. Of course, that is not always the case, but there are enough stories from every family to establish this statement as a maxim.

Hoping to disprove this theory (to protect my

own reputation!), I phoned my mom one day. With my "oldest and dearest son" voice, I coaxed her to give me some examples of how responsible I was as a child. The silence on the other end of the connection worried me a bit, so I ventured an easier question: "Did I ever show any small signs of irresponsibility, Mom? Think hard, I know it will take you some time, so you can phone me later if you . . ."

"No dear. I can think of many things. Are you prepared to take notes?" And off she went, describing time after time when I acted less than competent.

Again searching for affirmation of my capability as a youngster, I asked her, "Mom, when did I start cleaning my room to your satisfaction?"

"Come to think of it," she said, "it was about the time you got married. You can thank Kathy for me."

I knew she was right about me. After all, I was a child. But Mom and Dad did all they could to instruct me to act responsibly. Despite their attempts, though, my siblings and I tried to shuck our responsibilities as a snake sheds its skin. Responsibility cramped our style.

For instance, Saturday mornings at our house could be great, or they could be . . . My sister always had a theory about Saturday mornings: If Mom had curlers in her hair, we were in trouble. And the tighter the curlers were entwined in her hair, the more fiendish the plot she had devised for us.

Sis maintained that it had to do with her hair being too tight. I'm not sure there wasn't truth in that theory!

Mom worked all week, and we were expected to pitch in with the daily chores. Monday and Tuesday she had enough energy to chase after us three freeloaders to make sure the house remained livable. By Friday, she was exhausted, and we were defiant. This combination created a volatile mixture—a mixture that often exploded on Saturday mornings.

Mom would get just enough sleep to be dangerous—to us! As we figured it, just when she began to wake up, the thought of our negligence during the waning days of the week began to bubble in her brain. She mentally recited to herself all the chores we were going to tackle that day, whether we liked it or not. Speaking now as an adult, I realize that she had a perfect right to expect us to be responsible enough to maintain the house while she worked to help support us. However, as a kid, I wanted no part of it!

By the time she got up, she had everyone's morning chores well mapped out. The curlers played the part of the barometer in this responsibility training exercise. Since she was in a rush to get the Saturday morning work done, she would put curlers in her hair to put off fixing it up. The tighter the curlers, the more aggravated she was. Or so it seemed.

The point of this has to do with my father's actions during these conflicts. He loved to repose in bed on Saturday mornings. At the time, I never thought much about it, but I now can see that his absence was my license to be more defiant than I normally was. After all, he set the example of how I should behave.

As the strongest member of the family team, the father must be the anchor in the tug-of-war against anarchy. If Dad doesn't participate in the rules of responsibility, there will be renegades in the junior ranks.

The Garden of Eden is a choice starting point in the understanding of a father's part in responsibility training. Adam opened his eyes to a garden of delights (the word "Eden" means "delights"). The perfumed fragrances tantalized his senses, filling him with joy and wonder. Then Eve exploded onto the scene, and once again Adam opened his eyes to a scene of delight. Together they stood in innocence and awe, trying to calculate the nature of the intense feelings they were experiencing.

Adam and Eve, though full grown, were mere children in their understanding and wisdom. They were presented with a plethora of possibilities, a chalice of well-selected choices to drink in. But in this idyllic crucible, the greatest battle of mankind's history was lost—and it seemed so easy. Satan confronted the couple, and they gave over the keys to their world. Our race was doomed, and sin gained mastery over creation.

Yet God made the garden. And as we look at His work, we see that it was intended to be a place of freedom and a place of responsibility training. It was meant to succeed, too. The perfect Father, in laying out the garden, also lays out for us a pattern that we can use to cut out our parental "garden of responsibility training."

Responsibility as seen by Father-God

The first few chapters of Genesis can seem disjointed if they are viewed in strict chronological order. Actually, the events of Creation are easy to follow until we come up to the making of man. The other parts seem to have no purpose. We are left to assume that they are brought into existence either at the caprice of God or for some unseen and untold destiny.

Not so with man. Genesis 1:26 says that man is to "rule over the fish of the sea and the birds of the air, over the livestock, over all the earth, and over all the creatures that move along the ground." God's grand plan called for man to be the ruler of the rest of creation. What a mandate to fulfill!

God even expands this charge: "Be fruitful and increase in number; fill the earth and subdue it. Rule over the fish of the sea and the birds of the air and over every living creature that moves on the ground" (verse 28).

This is man's job description, his mind-boggling mission for which God has prepared him. But . . .

Moses, the writer of Genesis, inspired by the Spirit, realizes that this grand command may be misleading. Though God has designed man to populate the planet and take care of it, He had no intention of everything falling into place on Day 8 of Creation's history. Though full-grown in stature and strength, man is ignorant of the world into which he was born ruler.

In fact, man is not ready to rule. Thus, in chapter 2, Moses steps back to reveal the initial steps that God took in order to teach Adam how to be responsible for earth. It didn't all happen overnight.

Genesis 2:8 presents the first pediatric training center: "Now the LORD God had planted a garden in the east, in Eden; and there he put the man he had formed." If man was the master of earth, why was God limiting his focus to this chosen area? The Hebrew word for garden reveals why God did this. It means a "walled-off area." God had prepared a training area, a veritable walled-off garden of delights. Verse 9 tells us that all kinds of trees grew there and that there was a center of this garden where two special trees grew: the tree of life and the tree of the knowledge of good and evil.

Why did God limit man to the garden? Why not strap a satchel to his back and send him off to track through the new world? The answer is simple: God is a Father, and as such He wants His children to take their chosen responsibilities slowly—even painfully slowly!

Verse 15 says, "God took the man and put him in the Garden of Eden to work it and take care of it." When man showed God he was good at horticulture, God moved him on to zoology. Verse 19 tells us that God brought all the animals to man to see what he would name them.

From the next verse, we can assume that Adam

fulfilled this task faithfully, which leads me to the point that the first focus in responsibility training is knowing how much responsibility to give a child. And the second point must then revolve around when to increase the level of responsibility and by how much. Father-God's pattern speaks explicitly to these questions and lets fathers know that *less is more*. Helping a child to gradually adapt to his obligations in life is much better than throwing him into the fray inexperienced.

I recently read a tragic story in the newspaper. The headline read "Boys Burned in Blaze." A local father had decided that it was safe to leave his five- and two-year-old boys at home alone while he went to the hospital to pick up his wife and third son, who had just been born. In his absence, the two boys somehow started a fire. The older boy died; the two-year-old is still in the hospital, receiving critical care and skin grafts.

The horror of this conflagration underscores the lesson that God is teaching in the Garden of Eden: Give out responsibility carefully! No five-year-old is capable of baby-sitting.

Allow some bad consequences

The garden had only one menace—the tree of the knowledge of good and evil. The rest of the garden was not extremely difficult to care for, so it should have been an elementary lesson for Adam. But the off-bounds tree was also part of the basics of responsibility training. God would never have placed it in such a central spot if it were not essential to spiritual growth and mental acumen.

And here is the third rule in training children to be responsible. Children must be given opportunity to practice proper actions *as well as* the opportunity to abstain from harmful things.

We must not shield them from *every* bad consequence. God could have left out the tree of knowledge of good and evil. It still would have been an exquisite garden. Adam and Eve wouldn't have known the difference. But God intended that there exist a potential problem spot—some area where man could choose to obey or disobey Him.

How are we to pattern our parenting after this? Surely, we should not suppose that God intends for us to leave random perils around our houses just to see if our kids will obey us. Common sense tells us that razor blades and rat poison have no place around preschoolers. But as our children grow, they should be given responsibility when their noncompliance may bring serious consequences.

Our kids want a dog. But Kathy and I are away for conferences and seminars on a regular basis, so we're not fond of having to find a baby-sitter for Rover as well as for the children. I have resisted all their attempts at trying to talk us into it—promises, crying tantrums, pleading and even pouting by my four-year-old. They even tried borrowing a dog to show me how well they could take care of one.

My wife is starting to crumble. A few months ago she was talking to me about the responsibility teaching we are doing with the two older boys. "Maybe a dog will teach them how to take care of something," she said.

"Dear, they won't take care of it—you and I will," I countered. Having said that, I knew I had closed the door on the discussion, because we both know that few children keep their promises when it comes to taking care of pets. My wife, however, was ready with a response.

"Well, let's start with goldfish. If they handle those well enough, we'll talk again about getting a dog."

So we bought some fish, one for each boy, complete with a bowl and food. My one cautionary rule was this: I would not feed their fish, and if they died because of starvation, that would be the end of pets.

So far the fish haven't done the graveyard back float yet. It looks great for the fish but not so good for me. We soon may be getting a dog!

Kathy got her comeuppance, though, when the boys wanted to make their own breakfasts. My wife is a "clean kitchen" fanatic, and therefore requires that anyone who cooks have a "parental union badge"! So when I suggested that the kids could fix their own breakfasts, she was not pleased. It piqued her sense of propriety to think that the kitchen she loved and worked in would have children running roughshod through it.

"What will happen to the kitchen?" she wanted to know. The worry lines knotted her face into confused shapes.

"There won't be that much of a mess," I replied, knowing full well that the opposite was true. "I'll help them clean up if there is."

My wife would not go along with the plan until I reminded her of the goldfish. She stood in silence, no doubt wondering how she could get out of this situation. Then she smiled one of those darling, little smiles that causes me to shiver.

"All right," she said, "but there are going to be some rules."

After rule 96, I stopped listening. Actually, there were only about 10, but they sounded much like the Ten Commandments. After she finished delineating the decrees, the kids quickly agreed to abide by them.

Rule number 11 was for me. If they made a mess, I was responsible either for making them clean it up or doing it myself. Who said responsibility training was all fun?

Responsibility has as its root the word "response." Each person has to learn how to respond to the challenges and roles laid upon him. The continual exercise of right responses is the greatest indicator that responsibility has been learned.

If we were catatonic robots with no ability to freely choose, responsibility training would be a simple, step-by-step procedure. The Garden of Eden not only exemplifies the kind of responsibility that God handed over to Adam and Eve, it also shows the various forms of freedom He granted.

Freedom as seen by Father-God

With the failure in the last several years of notable televangelists, the media has shown a propensity to scrutinize Christians and Christian organizations. No doubt some reporters are looking to break the "big" story, hoping to show the world that hypocrisy is rampant in our ranks.

Theoretically, we should be glad this happens. It keeps Christians considering both the eternal and the public consequences of misbehavior. In reality, though, most of us wince when these stories surface.

One such negative incident just occurred where we live. A Christian organization that runs a home for incorrigible boys was accused of wrongdoing. Labeling itself as a "tough love" alternative to therapy and institutionalization, the group made a reasonable case for its procedures and beliefs.

But what has come out about the organization indicates that its methods were far from reasonable. Its counselors have been accused of using cattle prods, abusive language, physical abuse and even torture to reinforce their system of discipline. Many boys who emerged from the program talked of a list of punishments that would be administered for even the most minor crimes. When interviewed, one of the directors stated that the way to complete freedom for these youth was the complete removal of all freedoms. When I read that story, it brought to mind thoughts of the Gulag prisons in Solzhenitsyn's books.

Freedom vs. responsibility

As much as mankind deserves to have every freedom removed, God is not willing to do it. He sets the pattern for this in the Garden of Eden.

Right from the beginning, God allowed Adam the freedom to be his own man. When Adam was given the garden to tend, God placed few restrictions upon him. We have seen that the only tree Adam was to leave alone was the tree of the knowledge of good and evil. The rest were his to enjoy anyway he wanted.

I can't imagine God lurking around the trunk of a peach tree spying on Adam, just waiting for him to slip up so he could remove his gardener's license. Nor would He create a new, revised list of instructions relating to the Agricultural Ministry every day. And God did not overrule any of the names Adam gave the animals. These were His son's offices, and the Father let him have a go at ruling this small piece of the planet. This is God's richest grace at work.

Was Father-God being naive in giving Adam this much room? Did He trust Adam so implicitly? I believe the answer is no to both questions. Trust has little to do with granting freedom. The Heavenly Patriarch does not base freedom on how much He trusts us. If He did, freedom would not exist. God bases freedom on His plan to see His freely choosing creatures choose the right way and, ultimately, follow Him.

This is not to say that God had no influence on

the choices Adam was to make. *Responsibility training* is the course of action that a child is slowly and deliberately guided into so that he will know what the proper course of action in a given situation should be. *Freedom* is what is granted to the child to see if he will be responsible on his own.

How different this is from the conventions of modern thought. A few days ago, I flipped through the television channels to see what was on. On one channel was the 1960s drug culture movie *Hair*. It drew me in with its psychedelic setting and its anachronistic script. Words like "groovy" and "right-on" and the inimitable "sock it to me" rattled my memory.

One scene showed a man who had recently been an "uptight" (another '60s euphemism) business executive who took his first LSD. He "grooved" into a love scene with the girl of his dreams. They flew around free as birds with a priest and church choir in a wedding scene floating right along. In that scene (both before and after the LSD dreams), the word "freedom" is used more than any other. To the pop sentiment of the '60s, freedom was both the absence of responsibility as well as the right to do whatever felt good.

The decades since that era have not succeeded in replacing this working definition of freedom. Sure, AIDS, drug awareness programs and some pop psychology warn us to be aware of the risks of unbridled freedom. Few modernists, however, even suggest that responsibility and freedom are compatible.

A talking snake

But Genesis 3 tells a different story. This passage will exist for all time as a message to humanity of where freedom without responsibility most often leads: to sin!

The garden had a visitor one day, something that probably surprised Adam, because God had not allowed any visitors into the nursery up to that point. In a sense, he was not really a visitor. Adam surely had seen snakes—he earlier had named them. But here was a snake who talked. Satan had been allowed to enter the serpent and give it the power of speech. This should have put Adam the zoologist on the defensive, but it didn't.

Let's clear up some misconceptions about the Great Temptation. First, an apple is not mentioned in this story, only fruit. Verse 6 also reveals that Adam was standing beside Eve through the whole scene. The phrase "who was with her" implies that Adam had heard every word the serpent said to Eve and that he did nothing to warn her. This is why *Adam*, not Eve, should be credited with the first sin. He saw through the lie and did nothing to stop the trickery. He sold himself and his wife into spiritual bondage and slavery by remaining silent.

Where was God while all this was taking place? Was He taking a meteor shower while the sin salesman came to the oasis to tempt His tykes? God absented Himself to do what all fathers must do—He was waiting to see if responsibility training would translate into responsible actions. In this case it did not, but we would be foolish to conclude that granting freedoms such as God did here is improper.

Proverbs 22:6 speaks of this principle in a way that may mislead us if we're not exact in our interpretation. It says "Train a child in the way he should go,/ and when he is old he will not turn from it." First, let's view the message here as a *probability* and not as an outright *promise*. Experience should tell us (as well as history) that this is not always true. Many children have grown up to be horrid when their parents were saints. And, conversely, some kids have emerged as saints when their parents were horrid. Given the laws of probability, though, a child who is raised according to a certain system of living will most likely adhere to it when he grows up. Notice that it does not necessarily happen when he is young. Only the most compliant children skip the phases of outward rebellion and slide smoothly into the mantle Mom and Dad have left them. Usually, this verse applies most accurately when children grow up to face the same kind of critical dilemmas that their parents faced.

Even though our children may let us down, we still are bound by God's example to give them enough freedom to see if they will act responsibly when we are not around.

Here's an example. Beginning at age three and ending at who knows what age, the telephone is a fascinating device for people. Long before we ever master the theories that make A.G. Bell's invention work, we love to try it out. Numerous times I have caught my children at a young age randomly dialing. My greatest fear was that the next telephone bill would have a five-minute charge for a phone call to Hong Kong! So I labeled the phone as off-limits and left it at that.

When our oldest son reached the ripe age of four, he used to race to answer the phone every time it rang. Since he would invariably beat me there, one of three things would happen: He would pick it up and stare at it; he would venture a shy "hello" and then say nothing else; or I would be close enough to grab it before it reached his mouth.

Many times he would cry, and his mother would have to soothe his wounded soul while I found out what the caller wanted. I reasoned that it was better this way. None of the calls would be for him anyway.

By age six, I noticed that he was becoming inordinately curious about the telephone, always asking to call a friend "just to talk." I sensed that my parental bill of rights was being tugged at, and I didn't want him to have the freedom of unlimited dialing. What was I to do?

The answer came when I called the home of one of our church members. A child answered the phone politely and said, "This is the Greer residence, may I ask who is calling please." At first I thought it was the family's seven-year-old who answered, so I commended the child by name. The child on the other end of the line instructed me that he was the four-year-old and could he "know who was calling, please." *I* don't even have telephone manners that proper.

What I realized later is that I was averse to handing out telephone privileges because I had never taken the time (as this family had) to teach telephone responsibility. This is often the fear that grips the cockles of most parents' hearts. They know that their kids are not well trained, so they cannot grant freedom. But there is another answer: Teach them!

Since that call, I have sat the kids down, one by one, and gone over the procedures for answering the phone. They're taught what to say when we're not home, how to deal with a prank caller, how to handle a call from a stranger and how to answer someone who wants more information. The more we taught them, the more I realized how much needs to be learned about a simple thing like a telephone.

As I scan the Bible, I see that God was always willing to teach responsibility *and* to grant freedom. I think of David as king, Joseph in Potiphar's house and Paul waiting blind in Damascus. For each of these men there was much training. And each was granted freedom to choose the path he would take. Joseph, in choosing to be pure, went to jail. And from jail he went to being a ruler. Paul, though blind, was offered healing and service in God's Kingdom. David could have chosen to stay with the Philistines, but instead chose to become king of a nation that did not appreciate him.

God is not threatened by granting freedom to His

children. But we usually are because we have not effectively communicated responsibility to our off-spring.

As a pastor, I am often asked by parents how old a child should be before he or she is allowed to date. A number of good books are available on the subject, each with its own idea of the correct age. But I believe that age, though important, is only secondary to the freedom-responsibility question.

I have frequently asked parents if they believe they have adequately taught proper attitudes concerning sex and its responsibilities. If they respond affirmatively and if the youth seems socially and biologically mature enough to begin this stage of life, I usually counsel the parents to give their teen a *measured* amount of dating freedom. I say measured because this freedom is best appreciated when handed out in small but regular quantities rather than in heaping helpings.

Conflict as seen by Father-God

The first 10 amendments to the Constitution of the United States are by common assent referred to as the Bill of Rights. As such, they are a guarantor to all citizens of the United States that the freedom they enjoy shall not be impinged upon by the government of the land—no matter how much the government may desire to do so.

As you examine these "guarantees of freedom," one thing stands out: someone expected trouble ahead. *Conflict* is the underlying current in the first eight articles of the Bill of Rights:

Article One speaks of "prohibiting" and "abridging" and "redress of grievances."

Article Two talks of "security of a free state" and "right to keep and bear arms."

This pattern continues through Article Eight. My point is this: Wherever a man speaks of freedom, in the next breath he must take into account the existence of conflict. Freedoms often collide, resulting in conflict. This began in the Garden of Eden and has become intensively more complicated since then.

God is the ultimate Free Agency. His freedoms will forever remain unrestricted, for there is no power in existence that can argue with His will and successfully oppose His right to do as He wants. Adam and Eve exercised their freedoms up until the time they stepped into the area of prohibition. And when they did, conflict arose.

Then the man and his wife heard the sound of the LORD God as he was walking in the garden in the cool of the day, and they hid from the LORD God among the trees of the garden. But the LORD God called to the man, "Where are you?" (Genesis 3:8–9)

On one side was God, whose freedoms are universal and unassailable; and on the other were Adam and Eve, whose freedoms were limited and granted with certain restrictions. They had crossed the boundary of the freedom and therefore were bound to lose it.

We make a mistake by viewing the remainder of Genesis 3 as God's punishment for Adam and Eve's sin. God had already stated explicitly what the punishment for sin was: death. Genesis 3:11–24 does not describe punishment but the revocation of certain freedoms as a result of overstepping the stated boundaries.

Look closely at these verses and see how the natural freedoms of the new world are now irrevocably denied Adam and Eve.

> 1. The freedom from spiritual warfare—revoked in verse 15.
> 2. The freedom from pain and ease in procreation—revoked in verse 15.
> 3. The freedom of egalitarian family life—revoked in verse 16.
> 4. The freedom from toil–revoked in verse 17.
> 5. The freedom to command the earth—revoked in verse 17.
> 6. The freedom from weeds and destructive forces—revoked in verse 18.
> 7. The freedom from physical deterioration—revoked in verse 19.
> 8. The freedom of innocence—revoked in verse 11. (They knew they were naked. Shame in their spirits was reflected in shame at their nakedness.)

When freedoms collide as freight trains on the

same track, there will always be a mess. And when a child abuses his freedom, the clear answer must always center on removing the freedom until responsibility is once again taught and confirmed in the child.

Lost tickets

As a teen I had saved for months to attend a Stampeders (a hot Canadian rock group) concert and waited in line four hours to purchase tickets. Their guitarist played a double-necked guitar, and I, a budding guitar aficionado, was enamored with his style. I was eagerly looking forward to hearing him play.

Everything was set. My brother, Dave, was going with me, and we had lined up a couple of dates. The final part of our plans consisted in our father's willingness to drive us to the event. Nothing could go wrong. Or so we thought.

Dad dropped us off a couple of blocks from the auditorium. (After all, it wouldn't be cool to have your father chauffeur you.) We wandered up the stairs and reached for our tickets. I found mine quickly and prepared to dart in the door. I glanced over at Dave to see a ghostly white expression creep over his face. He had lost his tickets!

He searched in every pocket, but they were nowhere to be found. I panicked internally, weighing my options. I reasoned that I had worked hard for my tickets. I was free to do as I wanted. My brother could do as he wanted. Even though our father had told me to take care of David, my brother wasn't a baby anymore. I almost skipped the concert, until I looked at the face of my date.

I left David on the steps and went into the concert. He and his date foot-cruised to the corner grocery store and called my dad to give him a ride home. I heard later, when I showed up at the rendezvous spot, that Dad had been quite perturbed when he arrived to pick Dave up. By the time he came to get me, he was livid!

After the two-hour lecture, Dad assured me that this would never happen again. He was right. Dad never drove me on another date. He never again gave me that responsibility. And in a seemingly unrelated turn of events, that girl never went out with me again. I don't think my earthly father had anything to do with that—it was a result of my stupidity.

Inasmuch as freedoms should be granted when responsibility has been taught, so freedoms must be restricted when responsibility is not maintained. These two always seem to travel in tow of one another. You can't have one without the other.

What can we conclude? Responsibility without freedom is ungodly bondage. Freedom without responsibility is unbridled anarchy. A father's freedom supersedes the desired freedom of the child when freedoms conflict. Finally, a freedom abused is a freedom denied. Fathers must deny freedom when a child proves he has not comprehended the scope of responsibility.

One father is more than a hundred Schoolmasters.

—George Herbert

A man finds out what is meant by a spitting image when he tries to feed cereal to his infant.

—Imogene Fey

Chapter 6

Teaching a Skill

M ama, Mama—I can do it!" Our little boy came steamrolling onto the small deck where we were having a refreshment break. In his delicate hands he carefully cradled an almost-full can of soda, making my wife and me instinctively want to grab the can away from him before any of it spilled on his grandparents new veranda. But we could see by his steeled expression that he had a death grip on the can.

"What can you do, John?" I asked. He raised himself up to full height and stuck out his chest with pride.

"I can drink with a straw!" he announced. "Uncle Glen showed me how." Then as if we were still neophyte unbelievers, he guzzled and slurped up as much liquid as his mouth could hold. We watched his cheeks expand until they looked like they would explode. Then when he had sucked all he could hold, he downed it in one gulp.

If you've ever swallowed a carbonated drink that way, you'll know what comes next. He looked shyly up at his mother, and with a grin touching the corners of his mouth, he said softly, "Uncle Glen showed me something else, too." Then he paused in a way not unlike a boxer ready to unload a stiff right hook and let go a gigantic burp! Kathy and I both reacted at once, though with vastly different comments.

I said, "John, that's disgusting."

"Where's Glen?" Kathy said, "I'm going to kill him."

And off she went to commit Unclecide. When she was gone, I told my son not to burp like that again in front of his mother.

If I had known then what I know now about the male members of my extended family, I never would have let any of them close to my boys!

My brother taught my youngest son how to spit, and how to make it hang together for better distance. My father-in-law passed on the time-honored and hallowed family tradition of making rude and annoying arm pit noises. Kathy's brother showed my sons how to make even more delightful sounds using their lips and their arms.

They have also showed them more innocuous skills such as drinking directly out of a carton of milk, eating cold pizza for breakfast and screaming at the top of their lungs when their favorite football team scores a touchdown. None of the family members have ever charged anything for these skills they have passed on.

Nor would I pay them if they had!

The passing on of skills from parent to child is not as simple as the above pseudo-examples. Great thought and effort must go into every attempt at skill teaching and acquisition. The most meaningful skills that human beings must learn are also the hardest to pass on. Loving, nurturing, achieving, sustaining, rebuilding, dreaming and working are all processes that, by their nature, require hundreds of attendant skills. We may even give up, as some parents have, and assume that certain skills are attained by experience rather than by modeled behavior.

"He never taught me nothing"

Gaston grew up knowing two things about his father: first, he worked hard to support his wife and kids (he told them this daily); and second, the first thing was all he knew about his father. He told me that when he was in trouble at school, he would go to his dad for advice. But his father only got angry at him and told Gaston to leave him alone.

For years Gaston was segregated from his father. His mother tried desperately to bring her husband and children together, but he never would have much to do with them. The man was a closed book. Gaston related one incident that later became monumental to his well-being. He asked his father where babies came from and how they were made.

His father's answer was a slap in the face: he was told that he wasn't supposed to think about those things. As he entered puberty, his urges were as powerful as his mind was ignorant. As a result of this, he allowed himself to become involved with a group of boys who would regularly abuse him homosexually. When he tried to speak to his dad about the matter, he was shoved away.

Years later, when I was helping him pick up the pieces, he would often cry profusely. In his tears, he would mutter a salty wish that his father had done something to help him grow up. His most bitter moment came prior to his complete healing. He looked at me with eyes that were distended and red from crying. With a look of utter hatred he said, "He never taught me nothing—not one bloody thing!"

What a sad and tragic story. In the field of responsibility training, a parent is grooming a child to learn the value of the proper responses in life. The ultimate goal is to bring a child from ir-responsibility to the point where he will act with intelligence and wisdom. Skill training does not look at an *irresponsible* child; it sees an *untrained* child. Its goal is to set down standard operating procedures that will adequately aid the child in living life successfully.

In Gaston's case, the father passed nothing down to his son, not even the barest scraps needed for survival. Since the family structure prevented

Mom from being helpful, Gaston was on his own in a hostile world.

Daniel Asa Rose, in a brilliant essay on the meaning of fatherhood called "Spring Training," says this:

> For two and a half decades, my father stood in as mankind to me. Whether he knew it or not, I invested mad amounts of energy both battling and celebrating this figure who seemed single-handedly responsible for making the world as imperfect as it was, and occasionally as fine.

In Rose's description of life with his father, he pictures a scene where the rest of the world falls back as a relief background and real life exists in the battles and blessings of how his dad tried to direct his life. Now Rose is the father, and he wonders about his own son:

> Now it's I who personifies history to my own son. This whippersnapper who steals second base watches me with hawklike brilliance, obsessing over my shortcomings, marveling at my occasional displays of wit. Now when I press Marshall's reluctant fingers on the piano keys, it's not because I think the baroque is great but because how else will it be passed down. Now when I put my teenage trophies in his room, I do it not to dwarf him but—so obvious!—to give him someone to look up to.

Indeed, how does anything get passed down unless the fingers of the father are pasted upon those of his child. There is no replacement for the moment-by-moment mentoring that a father can give to his children. Even when he is tired, there are skills to be taught about the proper ways to handle and view rest and recreation. To a child, the whole world is distilled into the details and grand motions of his dad's life.

Jesus puts this truth succinctly when He describes His relationship with the Heavenly Father in John 5:19: "I tell you the truth, the Son can do nothing by himself; he can do only what he sees his Father doing, because whatever the Father does the Son also does." The universe revolves around Father-God, and the Son of God is acknowledging that there is no one better to observe than the skilled Father at work.

Father-God is the perfect model in the realm of skill acquisition. John 5:20 goes on to say, "For the Father loves the Son and shows him all he does. Yes, to your amazement, he will show him even greater things than these."

There we have it. This is the template of true skill teaching. Father-God loves His Son. He takes the skills He possesses and, in an ever-increasing way, displays them carefully so the Son can copy them. As followers of God, our human fathering must begin with the assumption that true love seeks to prove itself in the teaching of skills in every facet of life.

While gathering material for this book, I happened to have dinner with my brother who, at the time, was doing a family history for a course he was taking to get his master's degree in family counseling. Without knowing it, his questions caused me to think of an experience with our father. At first glance, I thought Dad had been unnervingly negligent in this arena of skill training. But as we reminisced, we both came to a fresh appreciation of the volume of life he had passed down to us. Quite apart from mere genetic throw-overs, we have gained much from our father. And the more I think about it, the longer the list of skills that can be traced to him becomes.

Some of these I've included in the next few pages; most I have not. More important, what's delineated here is a bare outline of where God has brought His children through the ages and where human fathers can and should journey with their children.

Bathroom skills

Skill training starts early, almost from the moment a child is born. Does that sound ludicrous? Lydia Dotto, in her recent book *Losing Sleep*, cites several scientific studies done on the sleep patterns of newborns. The conclusions of the studies confirm that a parent can begin training a child to sleep through the night from the first night after its birth. Though a baby does not develop a sense of circadian (a 24-hour period) cycles until he is three or four months old, he is still able to comprehend what is expected of him during waking and sleeping patterns.

My wife, a licensed practical nurse, has a theory about nocturnal sleeping that has proven successful with our kids. After working in pediatric and obstetric wards, she observed that most babies are bathed during the night shift rather than during the more hectic moments of the day. Therefore, these tykes were being deceived into thinking that the night part of the cycle was for being awake.

So Kathy requested that the nurses not wake up the babies at night; she would bathe them during the day. After coming home, my wife and mother-in-law took turns getting up with each child as they aroused during the night. Instead of milk, they fed them water (which they also need, by the way). Our first son slept through the night after one week. The second and third children were not as compliant, but after a month they both snoozed at the prescribed time.

Please note: This is not the Phillips Proven Theory for Newborn Care. See your own doctor and do your own thing. The point is that even a newborn can be trained to follow the basic skills of life.

I call these elementary habits "bathroom skills," because a good majority of life's essential lessons revolve around the toiletries. Brushing of teeth, combing the hair, washing faces and lifting the toilet seat are essentials that no parent would think of leaving untaught. Other issues might include dressing one's self, what to eat, when and how much to sleep, how to talk on the telephone, how to walk and how not to leave gum on the chair when Daddy is sitting down to write (a very recent lesson).

God is not above teaching these kinds of things. In Genesis 3:21 He does His first fatherly deed for His children after sin has entered their lives: "The LORD God made garments of skin for Adam and his wife and clothed them."

Though this is not a favorite memory verse, the message is significant, especially when we consider that it was the first thing God taught man after the Fall.

God could have sat Adam down and begun training him in theology, reading, sociology (there was coming a "socio" to "ologize" about) and any number of useful curricula. But instead, He sat His son down and showed him the fine art of tailoring. We have to assume that God did more than just make Adam a set of clothes. Adam had to learn quickly that if he was to survive in a world where heat and cold and even shame abounded, clothes were necessary. God also relayed another principle to his son: *Basic living was going to be hard.*

Matthew 6:31–32 has this to say about our basic needs:

> So do not worry, saying, "What shall we eat?" or "What shall we drink?" or "What shall we wear?" For the pagans run after all these things, and your heavenly Father knows that you need them.

While this is a popular portion of Scripture, it can be misleading. Apart from manna and a few group feeding parties that Jesus hosted, it seems that God doesn't *just give* us the essential things in life; we must expend effort to get them. I think this indicates that our Heavenly Father will do all He can to ensure that we are trained properly in the acquiring of the essential skills in life.

That is why God created the family. In essence, it would forever be Adam's responsibility, and every father's who came after him, to systematically impart the initial living skills to his children. God showed Adam the most necessary skills: making clothes and obtaining food from the carcasses.

Drill sergeants

Are the "bathroom skills" worth talking about? It seems so incredibly obvious that a child has to learn to eat, sleep, walk, talk and hang up his coat on a hanger. Yet there are good parents everywhere who assume these skills should just arrive by something akin to a spiritual courier service. We say things like "Where is your head at?" and "How can you do that?" These rhetorical questions suggest a child should know something that we have never adequately taught him.

For most children nothing comes naturally. They are given to us as bundles of utter chaos and inexperience. Acting as proverbial drill sergeants, we must whip them into shape. The war we're getting them ready for is life.

My stepfather and mother have worked in a

group home for the mentally handicapped. I also have had several close friends who worked in institutions that cared for the mentally disabled. When they have described their duties to me, I thought their work must often be unpleasant—and futile. Teaching a 30-year-old how to tie his shoes, or an 18-year-old how to go to the bathroom, seems to me to be the height of hopelessness. Yet Mom and Dad's example of working in a group home has communicated something to me of extreme importance. If you take the time, effort and loving care to keep teaching a "bathroom skill" until it is learned consistently, even the disabled person can function in our world.

But the reverse is true as well. Even the brightest child, if given inferior training in the essentials of life, can be severely disabled in dealing with normal living conditions.

This is hard to admit, but one thing I never was much concerned about was body odor. My own odor never bothered me, and I guess my mother felt it was not her place to say anything to me about it. Oh, she would occasionally wave her hand in front of her face when I was near her, but I concluded, as did many of my friends, "That's just Mom." I loved Dad dearly and know he did his best to be part of our lives, but when it came to the essentials in life, he never said much. As a result, during puberty's sweat-producing years, I had many embarrassing moments that I didn't know enough to even be embarrassed about.

One day after French class my ravishing teacher

took me aside. I thought she was going to praise my good grades. Rather, she told me that I wasn't cutting the grade—socially—and that several of my friends had asked her to speak to me about my underarm odor.

She mentioned deodorant. My mother had bought me a can and regularly encouraged me to use it. But I didn't think it was necessary.

"Miss Gorgeous," the French teacher, burst my balloon. That day I went to the store and invested in a new can of scented deodorant. Only once, when I was too broke in college to even afford deodorant, have my precious pits gone without. Who knows, I may never have gotten close to being married if it were not for my French teacher!

Father-God didn't mind getting down to the basics. He probably explained to Adam why this kind of clothing was necessary. Human fathers should take a hint and on a sheet of paper list the elementary skills that go into living in this world. Then they should check off how many their children have mastered. The rest of the list is your challenge as a father to teach to your children.

Brotherly love skills

The prophet of God sat down wearily on the rock. The toil of watching his people decimated by war and ruin was hard enough for any Israelite to bear. But because he was God's man, others turned to him for an answer in the midst of annihilation. However, there was one problem with their expectations.

God wasn't saying anything! While mothers clutched dead infants to their bodies and sons cried to heaven for their fathers who lay in fractured heaps at their feet, Jonah only received silence as an answer to his desperate petitions. He could not comprehend how God could allow His people to be treated with such ferocity by the Assyrian invaders. It was a dejected man who dawdled by the road that day, perhaps feeling as if his Father in heaven had rejected him most of all.

"Jonah," an inner voice called. "Jonah, I must speak to you, son. Will you listen?" The inner compulsion he had always comprehended as God's voice now shouted urgently within his mind. *Here is the answer we've been waiting for,* he reasoned as he prepared to hear God.

"Go to the great city of Nineveh and preach against it, because its wickedness has come up before me" (Jonah 1:2). After that came the knowledge of His anointing resting upon Jonah, God's spokesman.

But unlike other missions the Master had sent him out on, this one did not fit well. He had no problem with the destination—Nineveh was ripe for God's judgment. They deserved a Sodom-and-Gomorrah-like cataclysm for the insane destruction they had inflicted. Jonah also didn't have much of a problem with the message itself. Not really. He knew that they needed to hear of the approaching doom about to explode in their midst.

It was the "40 days" he couldn't accept. He was not a sophomoric prophet who was unaware of

God's purposes. If God was sending him to preach a punishment yet 40 days away, then He had one prime objective in mind: He wanted them to repent! The thought of God offering forgiveness to those barbarians sickened Jonah. His rising indignation bloomed into both fear and abhorrence. Fear because God might not allow him any choice in this matter and abhorrence for God's plan that thwarted his thoughts of revenge.

So he made a decision—God wanted him to go east; he would go west. He quickly booked passage on a boat going as far west as the world went—to Tarshish, which literally means the end of the world. He wanted to be anywhere but in the midst of this plan God had devised.

Most of us could prosaically finish Jonah's journey. The sea comes to get Jonah through storms, sailors and a giant fish. After the fish spat him ashore like a beached barnacle, he was disciplined, chagrined and much the worse for having traveled the maritime route. Actually, though it came as small consolation to Jonah, his fish-belly experience would greatly help his mission to Nineveh.

What can we conclude from God's inventive way of veering Jonah back on His course? Obviously, no one can escape God's demands on his life. But does God really need to go to such exorbitant lengths to prove a point? The real reason God brought Jonah to Nineveh through such circumstances comes out in the final chapter.

In chapter 4, Jonah complained to God, "I knew

that you are a gracious and compassionate God, slow to anger and abounding in love, a God who relents from sending calamity" (verse 2). God needn't have wasted the mercy lesson on Jonah. He already knew all about it. That's why he took off. Jonah continued in his pity party and headed out of town to mope.

It's a typical childlike behavior and one that can result in serious consequences as it grows into bitterness. Father-God could not allow His son to give in to such resentment, so He enlists some *helpers* to teach the prophet a lesson.

He used the sun to "bake" Jonah until he was roasted. In Jonah's bleached-out condition, the heat would have been painful.

The Lord then used a vine to provide shade for our hero. And finally, a worm came and ate the vine, leaving Jonah where he started—hot!

Jonah feels God's presence and complains. God asks him if he feels his complaint is worth pursuing, and Jonah replies in the affirmative. Now for the punch line.

God said to Jonah, "You have been concerned about this vine, though you did not tend it or make it grow . . . But Nineveh has more than a hundred and twenty thousand people who cannot tell their right hand from the left, . . . Should I not be concerned about that great city?" (verses 10–11).

Because Jonah wrote the book, we can assume that he got the point, which is this: God wants to show loving-kindness and mercy and desires to teach His children (prophets included) that brotherly love is God's way.

As a father, I don the referee's cap more often than I care to. Why? To quell conflicts between our children. And believe me, I know from experience that sibling rivalry equals any multinational confrontation anywhere. In our house it always leaves my wife and me saying, "Why can't they get along?"

How does God model brotherly love skills? In short, He forces His children into relationship challenges. Examples of this abound throughout the Scriptures:

- Joseph and his brothers
- Isaac, Jacob, Esau and the blessing
- David and King Saul
- Ananias and Saul (Paul)
- The Greek widows and the apostles (see Acts 6)
- John Mark and Paul

In each of these cases, God orchestrated the events with precision so that the protagonists are faced with the choice of behaving in a loving manner or selfishly. In most of these cases there was a penchant for selfishness. But even when there was a retreat from brotherly love, God didn't give up on the training process. He waits a bit, then puts His children together again in order to see if they have learned the skills of loving others. No matter how many times Saul breathed out threats against

David, God kept bringing them back together. Despite the unthinkable cruelty Joseph's brothers did to him, God brought them together finally. Though Paul was disappointed with John Mark, God united them. (We even read in Second Timothy 4:11 that Paul said that John Mark became a "useful" and trusted companion.)

Treating mother properly

Recently, I took a week of vacation just so I could spend time with my family. We did jigsaw puzzles, read books, discussed science projects, played family games and did anything else the kids wanted to do (outside of watching television). We had a "togetherness" week.

By the second day we were all ready to do each other in. Competition in the games reached a feverous pitch. Our youngest child wanted to do something different every five minutes—just as the rest of the family was gaining an interest in a particular activity. Kathy and I wanted to do more adult things; the kids wanted to do more kid things. We were a mess, and I knew it.

I left the house intending to get some fresh air and tranquility. What I received was some great advice from my Heavenly Father. He pointed out to me that the main problem was that we were five people vying for each other's visual and auditory attention. No one was playing the role of referee or captain. It was a free-for-all family recreation explosion that was wounding the participants.

Arriving back home, I quietly began working to

change things. I took time to establish some family-time rules, then Kathy and I split up the team, with one of us reading and the other playing soccer.

But one of my sons continued to act contrary, especially toward his mother. I took him out for a drive and stopped at a park. I coaxed him into telling me some of the hang-ups he was having. He poured out his heart, and I listened. Then I pointed out some of his boyhood peccadilloes, and he agreed he needed to treat his mother with more respect. I had an idea, so I tried it out on him.

"Why don't you watch how I treat Mom, and you treat her the same way?" His visage brightened, and he expressed eagerness to try out this modeling exercise. After the week was over, Kathy commented to me that the two of them were getting along much better.

Every human being needs to be taught how to act in an unselfish manner. Selfishness is the core of sin's grasp over our being. Father-God's example points out the need to examine the social development of our children and to determine where selfishness needs to be curbed.

The ways parents do that are many, but God's favorite way is to put us in various relational arenas, and then give us the ways and means to work things out ourselves.

Employable skills

Leo Buscaglia, a best-selling author and public speaker, tells about the impact his father had in helping him choose a profession. Every night, his father would finish dinner and then stare at his children. They knew the question he was about to utter, for he had asked it every night. A favorite query was "What did you learn today?" The children could not plead ignorance; it was no excuse in the Buscaglia house. Those who occasionally tried this approach would be answered, "There is so much to learn. Though we're born stupid, only the stupid remain that way."

No fact was too trivial for the dinner table. If all they learned was the name of the capital city of Nepal, it was more than enough. Papa was satisfied.

When Leo migrated from home to the halls of higher learning, he saw how great a gift his father had supplied him with:

> When I finally emerged from Academia, generously endowed with theory and jargon and technique, I discovered to my great amazement, that my professors were imparting what Papa had known all along—the value of continual learning. (*Reader's Digest*, September 1989)

My father said it differently: "If you find someone who knows more than you do—and you will—pick his brains until you find out all that he knows." He would announce this to me often, for I had a major character flaw while growing up: I thought I knew everything.

Dad would often come home and read several newspapers from cover to cover. My most delightful memories of this presupper ritual were that he would often throw out tidbits to me. Long before trivia was in vogue, my father grasped the significance of the seemingly benign events that took shape around us. The stories he pulled out smacked of pathos, triumph and the human condition.

He often asked me what I thought of the story. He quietly listened to my opinion and then, without contradicting me, would sally forth with his version of the events. They were indeed eventful. He added color to the drab and pedestrian stories of average people doing archaic things. What I learned from these newspaper seminars was to be fascinated with people. It was probably by his side that I decided to become a doctor. People's diseases were an extension of themselves, and they needed excision—and study!

However, I never became a doctor. But not one bit of Dad's pedagogy was wasted. When God's call came upon my life to be a pastor, what stoked the burning fire was my desire to study people and their quirks. The Bible became a feast of foibles and follies, a tribute to the worst that man could be. My father's lifetime study of humanity was passed down to me in a way he nor I ever dreamed.

Without intending it, he gave me an employable skill. He imparted an instinct that all the institutions could not match. Part of the reason Dad's tutelage was so effective is that he went where no school can possibly go: to the beginning of my life.

In researching this book, I read dozens and dozens of articles and biographies relating to the way certain fathers raised certain (famous) children. Carpenters spoke of learning the love for building at their father's knee. Writers such as Buscaglia learned the quest for learning from their fathers. I read about performers who were challenged to create, painters who were coerced into seeing what no one else was seeing, missionaries who learned a decided love for people by looking at their patriarchs.

I am not just speaking of direct, transferable crafts when I refer to "employable skills." Almost anything that a father gives a child by way of a definable art or method can be used as a skill. My dad had no idea that his newspaper tidbits would build into me a habitual way of seeing people. But whether he intended it or not, what he gave me is used in my preaching, counseling, writing and even managing the church office.

God sets an example for this in the life of Moses. Most of us know the story well. The first stage of his life was as auspicious as it was dangerous. He was born in the middle of a deadly decree: all Hebrew boys were to be destroyed by the edict of Pharaoh. The king was afraid that the prolific Jews would out-populate the Egyptians. Moses' mother, not wanting to see her son murdered, sent him sailing down the canal in a reed boat. Sister Miriam was sent to watch what happened to the child. The story took an interesting turn at this point. One of Pharaoh's daughters, who happened to be sterile, picked up the basket and found the baby.

It was love—maternal love—at first sight, and the woman decided to adopt the boy. From that point on, Moses' lifestyle was that of "the rich and famous." We can assume that he learned great leadership skills in this household. All the while, he visited his real mother, who earlier had cared for him. We also can assume that she told him stories of his heritage, stories about Abraham, Isaac and Jacob. In these two households, God combined the love of the circumcised with the law of order and might. This became a potent combination.

However, before he was mature enough to be both leader and teacher of Israel, Moses tried out for the position anyway. He killed an Egyptian who was beating a Hebrew slave. Word got out to the authorities, and Moses fled the scene. So far his "employable skills" weren't much use.

Moses spent the next 40 years in the sheep business. The Bible doesn't tell us much about those years. But how much can you say? His diary would have been pretty scant.

In this tedium he put down his rash boldness and developed a calm, day-by-day attitude. When God came to put him into his real life's work, he was as humble as a person can be. Actually, he was too humble. It took miracles, promises and even an assistant prophet by his side to coax Moses on.

But Moses went, finally. And in the next 40 years or so, he was required to use all of his learned skills: the boldness of the ruler, the wisdom of a trained Hebrew, the patience and tenacity of a shepherd. Because he also had learned humility, he gave the glory to God.

God gave Moses every skill he needed to have an advantage in life. Human fathers can share the best of their abilities, hoping that some of them will be sufficient to use in making a living.

Transferring life-skills

I believe the secret is to take time to show our children all we know about the life-skills we are good at. For instance, my father taught me everything he knew about golf. He had spent many years perfecting his knowledge, and what he learned he passed on to my brother and me. He would teach us stances, grips, putting and hitting out of sand traps. He passed on etiquette, respect, grace in losing (sometimes) and the challenge to improve. It was one thing he did very well in life.

When he died, I stopped playing golf for 10 years. My brother, Dave, never did stop, and now he is an excellent golfer. But when I started playing again, the game had a different flavor to it. I was an adult, and I had to do more with this sport than just waste time at it. God has shown me two ways to use golf that have enhanced my ministry.

First, it is a surefire way to relax when things at the church are getting to me. I believe I've been able to live on an even keel because of God's ministry to me through golf.

Second, the game is a perfect setting for Christian fellowship. In the last year alone, I have established many contacts and struck up many conversations (with Christians and non-Christians alike) that have added to the effectiveness of our church's ministry.

Some of you may be thinking you don't have many skills—at least any that are of importance. But all of us learn hundreds of skills in the process of living life. If we pass each of these on to our children, then they will have an arsenal of techniques and knowledge that may combine together in some unique ways.

In the last two years, I have taught my kids gardening, football, guitar, singing, hiking, map-reading, writing and computer skills, how to change the oil in the car, how to cook omelettes, how to prune the apple tree, how to mow the yard, cement mixing, hammering a nail, how to use a photocopier, how to write a thank-you card, newspaper reading (a family tradition), how to exercise, how to kick a soccer ball, golf, Bible reading, tithing and how to take care of fish. My wife has taught them hundreds of other skills, too. I found that teaching these skills was relatively simple if I developed a plan. Here's what I found out:

1. Know what you want to teach.
2. Show them what to do.
3. Let them try it.
4. Show them how to do it better.
5. Let them try it again.
6. Keep showing them more intricate details.

7. Let them try it again.

I believe that God showed Moses so many examples of leadership styles because He wanted him to be the consummate leader. God modeled anger, compassion, loving care, rebukes and judgment. Then He let Moses try it himself.

Dating skills

For this delicate subject, we need to travel again to the Garden of Eden. In Genesis 2:18, we read about God's concern for His son Adam: "The LORD God said, 'It is not good for the man to be alone. I will make a helper suitable for him.' " God had made Adam so that he would freely and uncoercedly seek God his Father. It remains a mystery why God wanted man's company. But He did desire Adam's friendship, and He did His utmost to maintain strong ties. Did it make sense, then, to break up this solid, one-on-one relationship by creating a woman so shapely and desirable that she would draw Adam's head away from his Father?

In my amazement, I realize that God made the eventual sexual and spiritual union of His son Adam with Eve a *goal*! He invented them in such a way that they would want to be together.

Genesis 2:18 describes Eve as a "helper." The word "helper" is an unusual Hebrew word. Many translators have put forth the inherent ideas of partner, helper, assistant and aide-de-camp. But it's a word that suggests someone who comes rushing to your side in times of trouble.

If I were God, I would have sequestered Adam from anyone else he wanted to relate to. I would have prevented there being anyone else to relate to. But, thankfully, I'm not God. The main thought here, though, is that God is not threatened by Adam's attraction to Eve; He wasn't worried about the dating that would ensue.

Adam's first word when he saw Eve, translated into English, was "Wow!" Now God wasn't the only attraction in Adam's life. What causes me to take another admiring glance at my Heavenly Father is that He wasn't threatened by Eve. God could have invented Nintendo instead, and Adam wouldn't have been one bit wiser.

Let's take a hint from Father-God: Part of our job as fathers is to infuse our children with the excitement, knowledge and skills they will need to relate to the opposite sex. If at all possible, we should lay aside the feeling of threat and anxiety that attend the sexual area of our thinking. It is even proper to say that parents should give encouragement in matters of dating, sex and marriage.

It might be argued that God had the advantage of creating the perfect wife for His son. In addition, sin was not yet a figure in the equation, so perversion and aberrant behavior did not exist. Yet, notwithstanding these differences, it still could have been a threat to God to create a social force that had the potential of drawing His son away from Him. He took that risk and lays the gauntlet down for human fathers to pick up.

There are several levels at which dating skills can

be taught. The first involves knowledge. Our children should hear us speak about sex, dating and marriage. In the deluge of communication avenues open to our kids, much discussion centers around sex. If they hear it properly and first from their parents, then the misinformation from the media, schoolmates and pornography will not have as much effect upon their minds. To help in this, there are scores of reliable Christian books outlining the detailed steps involved in explaining male-female relationships to children.

The second level is the example stage. The father's greatest lessons on sexuality are often taught without him even being aware of it. How a father treats his wife and daughters will go a great distance in showing his sons how to behave around women. More than anything my wife and I instruct our kids by having them copy our actions. Around the house, Kathy and I are not private about our affection for each other. We embrace often, and our kids never seem embarrassed by our public displays of affection. We tell our children that we love them dearly, but that we love each other even more. They are not threatened by this; they assume this is what marriage is supposed to be.

The third level of dating skill acquisition training is the response level. Curve balls will be thrown at our children, and they will not understand the idiosyncracies of dating simply by our prior explanations. Fathers should be on hand (and willing) to answer the thorny problems that our children will encounter when dating commences.

My own father was not terribly helpful in this matter. He only gave me one piece of advice in dating: "Don't get anyone pregnant." That left a lot to the imagination. Though I followed his advice until I was married, it was probably due more to God's grace than Dad's counsel. I have resolved to do much more than this with my children. My sons already know how their bodies work, how a girl's body works, what sex is, why it is, how it is, when it is and other pieces of knowledge.

It will be several years yet before my first boy is ready to date, but he already knows the kind of girl he wants to date. In a recent conversation about girls, he said none of the fourth-grade girls interested him. I asked him why.

"None of them are as smart or good looking as Mom," he said. That's it son—hold out for the best! I may eventually lose a son, but in reality, I'll be gaining a "wow" for a daughter-in-law!

Spiritual skills

Our family was at the tail end of a summer vacation. We had spent a good part of it secluded in our favorite seaside resort just north of Vancouver, British Columbia, in a little town called Sechelt. The rich primordial forests offered miles of hiking trails and hallowed mysteries to explore. Above all, I had escaped the spiritual battlefield left behind me at the office.

The second to last day we spent there, I felt like giving my boys a spiritual lesson. Often when we hike, I like to use nature as my own personal parable-creator. As I thought about the beauty that surrounded us, the perfect analogy came to me. John, Andrew, Ruth-Ann, Meaghan and I trudged through the fern-lined path that led down to the ocean. On a bluff overlooking a small inlet, I stopped and had them sit down around me. *Surely,* I thought, *this is how Jesus felt when He taught the crowds on the side of the mountain.* I basked in the glory of my fatherly esteem for a moment longer, then jumped into my story.

"Look out at the water, kids," I told them. "It's higher than it was last night. Do you know why?"

They thought for a second. John, who likes to be first, piped in, "I think it is because the tide is in now and it was out last night."

"Correct. And why does the tide go in and out?"

"Doesn't it have to do with the moon?" Ruth-Ann wondered.

I told her that it was indeed the result of the moon's journey around the earth. Then I asked, "Why does God have the tide go in and out?"

They looked puzzled by my riddle, so I answered it myself.

"When the tide comes in, it brings new life and vitality to the shore. When it goes out, it leaves behind living things that feed the birds and make the seashore lively and exciting." Then I applied the point of my lesson. "This is what the Bible is like for us. When we read it each day, it brings new life with it, feeding us and leaving behind the possibilities of exciting and lively times with God as our Captain. Does this make sense?"

Three heads nodded up and down. But then I noticed that Andrew had a puzzled look on his face. He is reserved, so I coaxed the question out of him.

"Come on, Andrew—what do you want to ask me?"

"Well, Dad, if reading the Bible does good stuff for you, how come you haven't read it since we left to go on vacation?" It was all I could do to breathe at that moment. His question, which came across as a rebuke, was as hard to swallow as it was accurate. In my exuberance to take time off, I had flung God's Word aside as a piece of junk mail. As we walked back to the motel, I kept thinking of an answer that would justify myself.

I couldn't think of any. There wasn't any! In my ardor to be *heard* as the spiritual foundation of the house, I was negligent in my duty to be *seen* in that role. This goes against the prime directive in all good training—*show* more than you *tell*. If I want my children to read their Bibles, I have to read mine. If I want them to pray, I must pray with them. If I want them to help the poor, they must see me reaching out with compassion to the needy.

That evening I called a family meeting. I admitted to them that I had failed in not reading my Bible. I asked their forgiveness for trying to appear spiritual when I was not. We did a group forgiving and then a group hug.

"That's my wife's job"

Many fathers, even those who attend church,

throw off the mantle of spiritual teacher in favor of a less weighty title. They can be a football coach, homework checker and welding instructor, but when it comes to teaching children about God, they defer to their spouse: "That's my wife's department."

What is Father-God's example in this? Actually, the entire Bible is an accounting of how God taught His creation about spiritual things. Hebrews 1:1 says, "In the past God spoke to our forefathers through the prophets at many times and in various ways."

God takes every moment to pass on spiritual truth. But in case we get the erroneous idea that this is just God's job, look at Deuteronomy 6:6–9:

> These commandments that I give you today are to be upon your hearts. Impress them on your children. Talk about them when you sit at home and when you walk along the road, when you lie down and when you get up. Tie them as symbols on your hands and bind them on your foreheads. Write them on the doorframes of your houses and on your gates.

Notice how many verb-type words go into this spiritual teaching forum: impress, talk, sit, walk, lie down, get up, tie, bind and write. It is an active job. Look where it takes place: upon your hearts, on your children, at home, along the road, at bedtime, on your hands, on your foreheads, doorposts, houses and gates. In a sense, God is saying,

"Anytime, anyplace in any way you can, pass on what you have learned about God. Let your children know what you know."

When cancer attacked my father, he would not subject himself to the ignominies of hospital life. He wanted to be at home, sheltered in the comfort of the family he loved. Two and half months before his death, he finally met Jesus Christ the Lord. That meeting was as tempestuous as his life, and in a moment of faith, he surrendered his soul to the cleansing power of the Savior.

He was transformed that day. Mom read the Bible to him for hours at a time. When he wasn't sedated, he was hearing the Word of God and getting to know the Father he had neglected for 40 years. His wilderness experience came first in his life; now he had entered the Promised Land.

Approximately three weeks before he died, he asked me to come in and talk with him. He asked many questions about my plans for the future. Then he stopped and looked me in the eye.

"Mike, please remember something."

"What, Dad?"

"It's not easy to know God. It's much easier not to know Him. It takes work to know God."

"I don't understand."

"Mike, I wasted 40 years of my life not knowing God. I've learned a lot in two months because I had to."

He paused, then he said, "Mike, you don't have to waste time. Know God's Son now."

When I look at Deuteronomy 6:9, I add my own

commentary to the end: "When you're dying of cancer, don't forget to teach your children."

Tis a happy thing, To be the father of many sons.

—William Shakespeare

Chapter 7

"Adam, Where are You?"—
Fathers and Sons

The helicopter spun powerfully off the launcher. I followed it with my eyes as it headed in the direction of the Christmas tree. It nicked an ornament, then careened off in a new direction down the hallway, toward the bedrooms.

I loathed this house. The rooms offered nothing but ridicule and shame to me and my brother. I was afraid even to go near the bedrooms. But I fought off the fear and tiptoed after my toy. I had to have it; it reminded me of my dad. On his last visit to the group home, I tried to be brave and not cry. But I saw the tears forming in his eyes, and I could no longer control the ones waiting to appear in mine. I held him as tight as possible, wishing I could leave with him. I wanted to be with him more than anything. I still remember Dad wiping his tears on the sleeve of his winter jacket as he shuffled quickly out the front door. At four years of age, I could not comprehend why we could not leave this awful place. What had I done to deserve this?

I went back to the bedroom that I shared with five other boys and stretched out across the bed. Several minutes later, I was retrieved from my upper bunk. The woman told me my father was waiting for Dave and me in the living room again. When we appeared around the corner, there he stood with two parcels. He gave one to each of us and then hugged us for what seemed like forever.

My father cried again. They were quick tears, rarely seen, and never forgotten. Then he was gone—again.

Our mother had been diagnosed as having rheumatic heart disease and had to be hospitalized. For periodic stretches, we three children were taken care of by relatives—sometimes separated, sometimes not. One time, we were placed in a group home. It felt like months to my brother and me, but my mom assures me that it was for only a couple of weeks.

As I remember it, the group home had an enveloping sadness that wormed its way into the routines of daily life. All the children hated being there, but I doubt that the persons who ran the home were at fault. I was never physically abused, but there was this heavy pain the entire time we were there. Older kids taunted and ridiculed us. When I wet the bed one night, I faced the derisive comments of everyone when it was announced at breakfast the next morning.

After Dad left, I opened the package he gave me. In it was the toy helicopter. When its cord was pulled, the propeller would shoot off and whirl through the air. My brother was too young to make his work; but for me, that helicopter became my whole life. I can still remember it, though almost every other memory of that year being away from my parents, sister and home is a blur.

Why was that helicopter so important? It was the most significant thing my dad gave me to help me through that difficult time. I know now that it was a torturous ordeal for him. His thoughts were alternately on his dying wife, his job responsibilities and his own unique personal problems. He made sure we were cared for, but all we felt was the loss of our father and mother.

I would have risked death to hold on to that helicopter. It said one thing to me: My father loved me, and he was coming back for me.

For both of us, Dad's visits meant the world. He would wrestle with us and toss us into the air until we begged for mercy. We were boys, and he was the man we wanted to become. We needed him.

Dads make an impact

It is not trite or archaic to say that sons need their fathers. But today there is increasingly less solid contact being made between fathers and sons.

As a result, there has emerged a genre of teaching designed to downplay the significance of a father's influence on his son. Some psychologists have even suggested that a mother can adequately fill the shoes of an absent father (since sexual modeling does more harm than good).

I cannot agree less! Almost every single mother I have known has expressed grief at not being able to give her sons all they need. There is something unique that only a man can give a boy, and no attempt to appease the mores of our fragmenting culture can explain that away.

Newsweek magazine, in a 1990 cover article, explored the many facets and controversies concerning the differences between men and women. Physical differences aside, there is overwhelming evidence that men and women are biologically different in almost every way you can imagine. The controversies arose when they discussed issues of emotional, psychological, vocational and mental differences.

Much of the recent discussion involves which side of their brains men use most. It appears as if women use both spheres equally, whereas men take a sharp left turn off the center brain median when they think. I won't explain why this makes a difference (I'm not convinced that anyone has a definitive answer), but there seems little doubt that it does.

Other questions emerge as a result of these findings. Are boys more aggressive because they are taught to be this way or because it comes naturally? Do girls cry because they are allowed to or because they are made different from their male siblings? The argument rages on like a brush fire, while the differences remain.

There is another movement afoot in our culture that does not attempt to explain the differences but to exalt them. Recent books and articles have placed a new meaning on the word "sexuality." In the '60s, '70s and early '80s, sexuality referred to how much, or how little or just plain "how" you had sex.

Now it means who you are!

"Male sexuality" is often a pseudonym for everything that makes a man different from a woman. Much of this current discussion centers on maleness, since femaleness has been explored quite thoroughly by women's liberation literature. Several noted Christian authors have written books and essays celebrating the uniqueness of being male. Much is ballyhooed about the biological and genetic characteristics of a boy growing to be a man. These have been enlightening studies to me.

However, in the midst of this, it may seem less important to look at the man who helps a boy properly became a man. As much as I go along with the celebration of male sexuality as expressed in our biological diversity from women, I don't ever want to lose sight of the key element in the making of a man: Dad!

What do sons need?

The women sat in a semicircle at the restaurant,

sipping coffee and talking. I was waiting to meet a friend, when I spotted them—all women from my church. Remembering a message my wife wanted me to give to one of them—something I should have done two days earlier—I strolled over to their table.

"Hey pastor," one of them said as I approached, "I like the beard. I'll tell my husband. Maybe he'll grow one." At this, some of the others expressed dislike for my beard. Ignoring their comments, I pressed on with my mission.

"Kathy wants you to order some construction paper for Sunday school," I told the woman. "OK," she replied, and I turned to leave. Then one of the other women asked me a question.

"How's the book coming, Pastor? What chapter are you on?"

As we talked, I began to share some of my ideas on fathers and sons. Off went the top to the can of worms. For 15 minutes I listened to advice and anecdotes and even complaints about their sons and husbands. The number one gripe seemed to be that their husbands didn't seem to know what kind of impact they ought to have on their boys.

"My book centers on what God does as a Father," I explained, hoping that would be a sufficient answer.

"When you find out, tell our husbands," one woman said, "and do it before the book comes out!"

Their comments helped fashion this chapter.

The Bible has hundreds of examples of how God

treated His "sons." Studying these accounts was a unique experience and one that netted the clearest advice on things that needed changing in my fathering habits. The incidents chosen for this chapter are typical of the way God handled most of the men in the Bible. Yet be clear on this: Every boy is completely unique, and what must be done for one son will not be the same as for any other.

Building the relationship with challenges

Christian musician Don Francisco wrote a song a few years ago that speaks about God's encounter with Adam in the post-original-sin era. He called the song "Adam." In it, he musically portrays the Father walking through the Garden of Eden. His plaintive cry to His missing son is "Adam . . . Adam . . . where are you?" As the song progresses, it becomes the cry of God to all men: "Where are you, Adam?"

Genesis 3:9 confirms the content of Francisco's song. It says, "But the LORD God called to the man, 'Where are you?' " Did God not care where Eve was? Was Adam the only one who mattered? God could have called for the pair, but there was a unique relationship He had with His son. As much as some people would like to believe that God treats men and women alike, the Bible does not fully support this notion.

Of course, God forgives all people equally. He gives us all new life, and we all receive spiritual gifts. And obviously He loves men and women the same. But as our Heavenly Father, He does not train us and treat us the same.

When He came looking for Adam, we must assume God already knew what had happened at the tree of knowledge of good and evil. He wasn't watching the Bears and the Packers battle it out while Adam gave away the keys to planet Earth to Satan. Though He had withdrawn His presence for a while, in order to give Adam a free choice, He still knew what had taken place. Adam and Eve had sinned. God the Father had come into the garden looking for His son, not His daughter. His were angry, "Father" footsteps; He was not strolling down the garden path.

My kids and yours know what those footsteps mean when they hear them on the stairs. My feet go down heel first, making the most of the vibration to bring fear into wayward boys. I wonder what God sounds like when He uses His heels? I don't think I want to know. Adam, however, found out what an angry God was like.

God had left Adam in charge of the affairs of the garden. Notice that he was given headship of this place *before* the Fall occurred. Headship is not a result of sin—it marks one of the basic differences between men and women. God's challenge to His sons is that they must launch out and be leaders.

Notice in Genesis 3:17–19 what God says will happen to man on account of sin:

> Cursed is the ground because of you;
>   through painful toil you will eat of it

> all the days of your life.
> It will produce thorns and thistles for you,
>   and you will eat the plants of the field.
> By the sweat of your brow
>   you will eat your food
> until you return to the ground.

The pronouncement God delivered was that men were going to be physically stretched to the limit just to survive. We'll see in the next chapter that God sets challenges for His daughters, too, but of a much different nature.

God challenged His sons to achieve. He would not let them down by leaving them beaten and defeated. Though the world was now going to make it tough for them to scratch out an existence, God desired that His sons know that good, honest scratching is the ideal situation. In other words, God intends to work His boys hard.

Caring challengers

Jesse Jackson and his three sons were interviewed recently by *Ebony* magazine. All three boys told the interviewer how close they were to their dad. Their relationship was described as "respectful yet playful." They all were involved in their father's 1988 presidential campaign—and he worked them hard! He said that he expected more out of them as his sons than anyone else on the staff. In private they refer to him as the "Rev." But in public he always gets the epithet, "the Reverend." Though he is their friend (all three are in their 20s), he can be demanding.

The same issue featured an interview with Ken Griffey and his son, who both play for the Seattle Mariners. Though Ken Jr. has felt the pressure of his father's .300 career batting average, he says his dad helps him through it. Dad doesn't, however, go easy on young Ken. "We talk a lot about the game and the pressures," Ken Jr. said. Then he went on to tell how his dad pushes him to be a professional at all times.

Closeness and caring—yet demanding. This is the picture of Ken Griffey Sr., ball player and father. Young Ken Griffey mildly complained in the article that his father had been gone too often on road trips while he was growing up. But then he quickly added that Dad more than made up for it when he was home by playing the role of challenger in every facet of his life: school, sports and chores. He both demanded and modeled excellence.

Fathers carry more force when they lay down a gauntlet of challenge. This force consists of more than physical power, for there resides in most dads the innate drive to push their sons past where a mother would go. While sons need their mothers, especially when Dad pushes beyond sane limits, they cannot survive without their fathers' urgings.

Yet some fathers tend to want to smooth out the path for their sons. They had to endure difficult growing-up years and overcome them by digging in and getting the work done. When we have exerted "blood, toil, tears and sweat" to achieve a goal, we often desire to spare those who come after us the same arduous effort. We forget that the toil we faced is the glory we have attained.

Father-God set a lifelong goal for Adam with this challenge: "By the sweat of your brow you will eat your food." In other words, a man's ultimate satisfaction will be found in the victories that are won when the odds are set against him.

My sons are as normal as any other boys. They fight and compete daily for numerous prizes. These range from who will control the remote control for the television to who will make it upstairs to breakfast first. It annoys my wife, who wants everyone to finish first. I desire the same thing for my kids, but they are all going to have to earn the standing. I will not give it to them without a challenge. This is especially true for my sons.

Recently, I wrote four simple tasks on a mock racetrack and then hung this on the door. The track is marked out in 16 increments or slots. As my sons complete the assignments for that day (e.g. cleaning their room, 20 minutes of reading, good personal hygiene), I allow them to color in that slot.

Once the entire 64 slots are filled in, representing the completion of four different goals, they receive a reward for the effort. It usually is something they chose before that chart began. This last circuit through, my one son picked a pizza outing for him and a friend. Next time he wants 10 packages of baseball cards. After I had agreed to this reward, he worked diligently to complete the assignments that I had set for him.

We began this program several months ago, and I have noticed that my sons have exuded a greater aura of confidence and responsibility. They have also begun asking me if they can do extra chores. Though I explain they won't receive additional rewards, they still want to do them.

Placing the "pins" in the gutter

Spencer Johnson, in his book *The One-Minute Father,* tells the story of a man teaching his son to bowl. Before the lesson, he got permission to reset some of the pins. The manager, not wanting to offend a regular patron, agreed to this request. The man then walked down the alley and set two pins in each of the gutters.

"Why are you doing that?" the owner asked.

"My four-year-old son is just beginning to bowl. Where do you think he will throw the ball?"

"Likely in the gutter," the bowling alley manager said.

"Then that's where the pins will be." With that the man took his puny pupil and began the lesson. As the boy grew, he became more and more proficient at the game. When he grew up, guess what he became: a professional bowler! His name is Nelson Burton, one of the greatest bowlers of our time. When asked what his dad did to teach him the game, he said, "Because of Dad, I never remember missing."

What his father understood was that to a four-year-old, lifting and throwing a bowling ball was hard enough. He shouldn't have to worry about knocking down the pins, too. I can imagine there came a day when the boy was able to send the ball right down the arrows, and that's when all the pins came back on the alley.

First Corinthians 10:13 shows the example of the Father in this:

> And God is faithful; he will not let you be tempted beyond what you can bear. But when you are tempted, he will also provide a way out so that you can stand up under it.

Sons need to be challenged, just as temptations must come. But there are some challenges that would crush the spirit of a child. Limit the challenges, as Father-God always does, but beware of eliminating them altogether.

Building the relationship with confirmation

Two scenes taken from the life of Jesus display the second building block in a father's relationship with his son. The first scene takes place by a quiet river in a turbulent time. The other occurs on a quiet mountain in a turbulent moment.

In both cases God gives His Son a confirmation. The first scene is in Matthew 3:13–17:

> Then Jesus came from Galilee to the Jordan to be baptized by John. But John tried to deter

him, saying, "I need to be baptized by you, and do you come to me?"

Jesus replied, "Let it be so now; it is proper for us to do this to fulfill all righteousness." Then John consented.

As soon as Jesus was baptized, he went up out of the water. At that moment heaven was opened, and he saw the Spirit of God descending like a dove and lighting on him. And a voice from heaven said, "This is my Son, whom I love; with him I am well pleased."

Jesus burst into the scene that John the Baptist had created for Him. The Pharisees were getting nervous about talk of a Messiah who was about to appear. Herod was edgy when he considered the possible loss of his throne. John the Baptist was rising in popularity to the point that some believed he was the Messiah. It was a dangerous and confusing time. Jesus was on the hot seat: If He did not do things perfectly, the whole plan of God could be derailed.

Being the Son of God, He, of course, handled it correctly. He endured humility by being baptized, though He had done nothing sinful. He identified with sinners and humbled Himself before His Father.

You have to marvel at verse 17. God was not required to give a verbal answer to this act of obedience. He had sent the Dove as a sign that Jesus was baptized with the Spirit and would Himself baptize others with the Spirit. No mention was made to John about a voice. But the voice rang out, clear and true, announcing the heart's emotion that the Father felt for His Son: "This is my Son, whom I love; with him I am well pleased."

We find the second scene in Matthew 17. The disciples are anxious for Jesus to reveal His power and magnificence. They are bothered by His persistent teaching about His own death. And Jesus was dealing with the thought of being separated from His Father, a thing He would deal with until the last moments before His arrest.

He took His three favorite disciples and went up to a high mountain. In a previous chapter I explained the nature of this scene on the Mount of Transfiguration. Jesus is revealed to Peter, James and John as the Most High God. Moses and Elijah appear to Jesus—what they said we can never be sure of. Rest confident that the message was critical.

Then the Father makes the second public announcement about His Son. It sounds remarkably like the first, and in reality, it is the same: "This is my Son, whom I love; with him I am well pleased" (verse 5).

Why the same statement? It is no coincidence that these announcements occur at crisis points in Jesus' life. We can only assume that they were designed to meet a need that Jesus the man felt.

I believe Father-God was meeting His Son's need, confirming to Him that He was on the right track. Surely, you would say, the Son of God would know when He was doing the right thing. Is Jesus so insecure that He needed a pat on the back and a pep talk to carry His ministry through to the end?

Insecurity had nothing to do with it. Jesus knew the voice and leading of His Father, for He constantly heard His voice. Yet He lacked one thing that is decidedly separate from the need to be secure; He needed to hear that He was doing the job in a way that would be successful. God hid from His eyes the end of the matter. He knew of His death and ascension, but I don't know if He saw to the end of time. He did not know the day of His return, for example. No, He was not insecure, but He did need to know that His Father was pleased with Him.

Responding to successes

My wife picked me up from work one day and seemed especially excited to see me. I didn't have to wait long to find the source of her emotion. "You have to ask Andrew how he did in school today," she said. "He seems really eager for you to know about his day."

"What happened to him?" I queried.

"Well . . . I'm not supposed to say, but when I was in his classroom helping out, the teacher called both of us over. She told me he was working beyond the class in a special 'Whiz Kid' math program. He's been working on it for three days. Then she told us that he had completed all the work in the program—with no wrong answers. She says he's a math whiz, and she said it to him."

My youngest son is a shy child with an extraordinary sense of family togetherness. When there is a tear in the family fabric, he becomes moody. When the group is getting along, he is as happy as a lark. We don't hear many of his thoughts, but when we do they are usually accurate and thoughtful.

He is also my huggy-bear—he loves to hold on to me.

When I walked through the door, I saw him coming from the other end of the hallway. I braced myself for his jump—he took off three feet away from me—and I waited for the news I knew was coming. I felt like telling him I already knew what had happened, but something inside of me told me to wait for him to make the announcement.

"Guess what, Dad?"

"What?"

"Miss Hash says I'm a math whiz. She says I'm the best math guy in her class. She told Mom, too."

"That's great, son!"

Then he paused and fluttered his long eyelashes at me. "What do you think of that, Dad?" he asked. Since I'd already told him that it was great, I wondered what else he could be looking for. Then it dawned on me.

"You're doing great, son. I'm proud of you. You have always made me proud. I love you, Andrew."

When I got those last words out, he threw his arms strongly around my neck, capturing my chin in his chest. He held on for many moments until he finally released his hold. Then for the next half hour, he followed me around giving me more details of his math exploits. I know him well

enough to realize that he wasn't fishing for com-
pliments because of some vanity problem. There
was a great desire to be confirmed in what he was
doing. I didn't need to make anything up. I was
proud of his accomplishment, and I did not have to
embellish my joy at his work.

When Abel offered the proper sacrifice and Cain
did not, God refused to overlook the matter.
Today's "feel good" teachers would have ad-
monished God for confirming the actions of the
one and rejecting the offering of the other. Maybe
they would blame Cain's retaliatory actions upon
God's refusal to give confirmation. This is how far
we can stray from the truth when we do not use
God's example as the norm.

We are taught today that affirmation must be
given to children. Affirmation and confirmation
are similar, but not identical. Affirmation is the action of one person showing support and encouragement to another person, *regardless of their
accomplishment*. Confirmation is a statement of
support for what someone is doing or has done.
The two can sometimes be combined, but they are
not interchangeable.

On the night after my grandmother's funeral, my
Uncle Bill took me out for dinner. He had paid for
me to fly from Bible college out to the location of
the memorial service. We talked for many hours
that evening about my grandmother (his mother),
each other's lives and especially about my dad.

Dad and Uncle Bill were very close. When Dad
died, my uncle was the executor of the estate. We

shared our fondest memories of Dad until well after midnight. Then he caught me off guard with something I had never heard.

"Your dad used to brag about you and Dave going to church," he began. "He would tell me how even though he would have nothing to do with God, the two of you attended anyway. He was really proud of the stand you took for God."

I had never heard that from Dad. Even after he gave his heart to Jesus, he never told me he was proud of my Christian walk. How it would have encouraged me to hear those words then!

As a result of thinking about that, I take every opportunity to let my boys hear this from me. "You are my son. I am pleased with what you're doing. I love you." No greater gift can a man give his son.

Building the relationship with conversations

Eli left Samuel and exited his room with a sigh. If only his own sons would listen to him with the dedication and fervor of this young boy. Since Elkanah and Hannah had placed Samuel in his care, the lad had been ministering before the Lord, fully dedicating his attention to the work of the temple.

"Oh, Phinehas," he moaned, "why must you reject the commands of God?" Eli paused as a hopeless feeling swept over him.

Then he began the lament that had been the last thought of each day for many months. "Hophni, my son, will you not repent of evil and return to

Yahweh before it is too late?" Eli knew with a certainty that his two sons would no longer listen to his rebukes.

Another pang of guilt struck his heart as he recalled how he had been much too busy to direct his sons' moral upbringing when they were young and impressionable. He also recalled the prophecy a passing man of God had given to him: "And what happens to your two sons, Hophni and Phinehas, will be a sign to you—they will both die on the same day" (1 Samuel 2:34). He took one last glance at the sleeping form of this other young boy near the entrance to the temple's outer terrace—and the truth struck him like a lance. Samuel was his last chance to raise a son properly.

During the night, God turned up the heavenly loudspeakers and aimed His voice at the boy by the altar. "Samuel!" He called.

Samuel awoke. Having never experienced the authoritative voice of the Lord, he associated it with the only authority figure in his life—Eli. Quickly, he rushed to his master's side.

"Here I am," he said, out of breath. "You called me." It was both a commentary and a question. What could the old man want at this hour?

"I did not call. Go back and lie down." Eli answered.

Bewildered, the boy found his bedroll and lay back upon it. No sooner had his dreams begun when the same voice echoed in his ears: "Samuel!" it demanded. Again he left to seek Eli.

"I did not call you. Go back and lie down" was all

Eli could answer the inquisitive lad. Eli wondered to himself what might be stirring on this night. No sooner had he laid back down upon his mat when he noticed the toes of his prodigy at the doorway again.

"Here I am. I know you called me," Samuel said innocently. *Could this be the voice of God?* wondered Eli to himself. *Has El Shaddai passed the privilege of hearing His voice on to this young man?* There was only one way to find out.

> So Eli told Samuel, "Go and lie down, and if he calls you, say, 'Speak, LORD, for your servant is listening.' " (3:9).

For a while they both waited. Samuel waited with the inquisitiveness of a pilgrim about to launch his journey. Eli waited with the dread of seeing someone else going down a road he had once been steadfast upon.

Neither waited long. God spoke to Samuel.

Samuel could hardly have understood the full weight of the message from the Lord. Eli's house was being condemned, and Samuel was to deliver the message to Eli. The pronouncement was difficult, but Eli accepted it from God's hand, though it must have broken his heart. In Samuel, it had the opposite effect: It stirred his heart to keep hearing the voice of his Heavenly Father.

The cumulative effect of Samuel's devotion is recorded for us in one short phrase in verse 19: "He let none of [God's] words fall to the ground."

Every word God spoke mattered to Samuel, and God fulfilled every word He spoke to His son.

Another son of God, David, said it this way:

> How sweet are your words to my taste,
>   sweeter than honey to my mouth!
>   (Psalm 119:103)

> You are my portion, O LORD;
>   I have promised to obey your words.
>   (verse 57)

Jesus said, "For the Father loves the Son and shows him all he does" (John 5:20). There is a concept in God's Word of the Father holding a running conversation with His children. By this, the Heavenly Father imparts His point of view and priorities to His children who are seeking help in formulating a point of view and proper opinions in an ever-changing world.

Passing down opinions

I loved Saturday evenings when I was growing up. We would feast on the world's thickest and messiest hamburgers. Each of us would try to reproduce the hamburger sauce from the White Spot restaurant by combining every condiment in the refrigerator. Once I came up with a concoction that came close to the mystical sauce. However, I forgot to record the ingredients.

Added to the hamburgers were Mom's homemade french fries. They were so delicious that they would be devoured before the second batch was even ready. Mom never got any. My brother and I stuffed ourselves silly.

Then we would retire to the living room for hockey night on the television. Dad reclined in his favorite chair, and my brother and I sat at his feet.

As the game progressed, I echoed the color commentator, making my opinion heard after every significant play in the game. I also did something else that was even more telling than the comments. I would look up at my dad to see his reaction to what I was saying.

I admit that by the end of the second period, Dad would grow weary of my incessant comments. His answers to my commentary became increasingly terse. Sometimes it hurt my feelings when, by the end of the game, he would tell me to keep my mouth shut and watch. Now, as an adult, I realize he was trying to curb a problem I still have trouble with—I talk too much.

What I constantly was fishing for was my dad's opinion. Most of the time he gave it freely to me. When I was older, I learned defensive driving from his constant analysis of other people's skills—or lack thereof.

I formed political opinions from Dad's ideas. He maintained that government needed a balance of conservative fiscal policy with a healthy amount of social concern. Until this day, I can remember exactly how he felt about every major political figure of this century. He idolized Churchill. Though he felt sorry for the Kennedys, he did not like their rhetoric. Ben Gurion was a genius, and Truman was a puppet. All this I gleaned from Dad's comments.

Father-God also spent much time passing down His opinions on life, liberty and kosher cuisine to the children called by His name. Perhaps a monumental difference between God's opinion and my dad's opinion is that Father-God's opinion is law for everyone. My dad's opinion was only law when it applied to how I lived my life around him.

But the fact remained that a major part of our relationship revolved around *conversations* where he would pass down his view on life to me. And even though I do not fully agree with his views on politics, money or sports, I had a definitive worldview to hang onto until I had fully developed my own.

During 1990, the Right to Life forces staged a gigantic anti-abortion rally in Washington D.C. Though the secular press played down the importance of this event and predictably underestimated the number of people gathered along the Mall, there are few people on either side of the abortion debate who did not view this gathering as a major political platform.

One speaker caught my attention. He spoke words that had been in my heart for years: "They tell us that it's not proper to impose one person's morality on others. But someone has imposed his view of morality on 25 million aborted babies!" My point exactly! It is impossible (and undesirable) to believe that people should grow up with no opinions on life. All of us have, and need, the advice and mind-set of others when we're young.

In just one day, children are confronted with any number of opinions on any number of subjects— from condoms to "cold-filtered" beer, from abortion to the authority of parents.

As long as a running conversation is going to occur between kids and authority figures, fathers must play a major role in the exchange of ideas. Boys seem to need a great deal of input from their fathers, and girls seem to crave it from their mothers. In the interchange of ideas between a father and son, a male identity is transferred. If there is little conversation where the passing on of ideas occurs, then there will not be a transference of male identity. Instead, that identity will be taught by others.

A beer commercial came on the television not long ago. This is not unusual for a football game, of course, but the content of this commercial overstepped previous boundaries. In one scene a man and a woman are embracing in the shower, completely nude, obviously examining each others tonsils with their tongues. It was an erotic and titillating clip, and my two boys observed it before I could switch the channel.

When it was over, they both looked at me. Their look was quizzical and penetrating. Neither of them asked a question, but their eyes framed a query: "What do *you* think of this commercial, Dad?" I decided that it was time they heard a proper opinion on this sexual tomfoolery.

"I don't think they should show that on television," I stated.

"Why?" they both asked in unison.

"Kissing like that is not for other people to watch. That is the kind of kiss people do in private. There are public kisses, and there are private kisses." In order to underscore the meaning of a public kiss, I kissed them both on top of the head. Then in true manly fashion, they both jumped up and began to wrestle with me. For the time being, the television was forgotten. But the lesson remained.

A month later, we were watching the news when the same commercial aired. My wife had never seen it and was immediately upset by its graphic content. My youngest son looked at her and then blurted out, "They shouldn't show that on television."

His mother stared at him in wide-eyed amazement. Slyly, he turned to me and smiled with satisfaction. I didn't need to say a thing!

Building the relationship with confrontations

The bride's car pulled into the parking lot, and immediately everyone was tense in the foyer of the church. The 20-year-old groom seemed disoriented as he asked me what he ought to do next. Actually, I had sent him to my office until the bride had found her way to the place set aside for the bridal party. The groom had become over-anxious again and was standing right in front of the door his bride was about to enter. I tried to usher him back, but he was a hard man to move when he set his mind on something.

Carl, the groom, was a Marine. He was decked out in his dress uniform and for weeks had been as fussy as a mother-in-law about the wedding details. I liked him a lot, but he was driving me nuts. Now at a crucial time, he was getting in the way. On top of that, he wanted to stay right where he was. I could not persuade him.

At that moment his dad appeared at the back door of the sanctuary. Spying his son still standing in the foyer, he marched over and stood in front of him. I say *marched* because his father is also a Marine. And he, too, wore his dress uniform. Catching sight of his father, the young cadet automatically stood to attention. His dad spoke softly and succinctly; no one could have heard what he said as they stood toe-to-toe in their parade-best clothes.

Two things happened at once. Dad wheeled around and rejoined his wife in the front row. The son also wheeled around and marched crisply into my office—where he stayed! All through the service he remained calm and calculated, never losing the decorum that went with the uniform. He exuded an air of authority while following my instructions to the letter.

I've often wondered since then if every man should first be a Marine before he is a father. The man never used a loud voice; there were no threatening gestures. But there is no doubt in my mind that a powerful confrontation occurred. It was a confrontation where a father who was under control of himself helped his son get control of himself.

It may appear contradictory to talk of building a relationship with confrontation. But it really isn't, especially when we properly define confrontation. It doesn't have to be a situation where someone uses "fire power" to get a point across. Nor does it have to include conflict.

What is confrontation? It is two Marines, father and son, standing toe-to-toe resolving a dilemma. It is two lawyers pleading their cases in a court of law. It is Paul and Barnabas standing before each other in Antioch, discussing whether John Mark has what it takes to be an evangelist. It is bringing into the open what once was sealed behind closed doors.

A critical confrontation

The prodigal son left his father to attend the feast being thrown in his honor. He heard his dad praising God for the epitome of grace he had witnessed. He left his patriarch, confident that even though he had given up his inheritance, he would never lack for food and shelter under his father's roof. He left his dad, and Dad stood alone in the road.

The father watched his wayward son wander off to the party. Tears continued to flow as he thanked God for returning his son to him. But as he was giving thanks, he heard a loud noise behind him. It sounded as if someone was angry. But try as he might, he could not find the source of the anger. He quickly stopped looking and went in to join the merriment.

The first thing he witnessed was his youngest son regaling everyone with how good the food tasted. The boy described the slop he had been living on for months, and groans were heard throughout the room. At that moment, the prodigal caught sight of his father standing in the doorway. Tears flooded from his eyes and down his face as he picked up the earthen drinking vessel.

"I drink to you, master," he began. "I call you master because I must earn the right to call you Father again. You have shown love to me all my life, but this kindness is the greatest of all." Cheers were heard around the room as the boy and his father closed the distance between them and embraced again.

The party swelled and grew as neighbors and acquaintances came by to join the festivities. But one face was noticeably absent from the party. *Where is my oldest son?* the father wondered. He asked the chief steward and the husbandman to find him. They returned several minutes later.

"Master," the steward began, "your other son is outside."

"Well invite him in!" the master replied.

Both men shuffled their feet. No answer came from their lips, and neither man left.

"Well, what is it, friends? What's wrong?"

"He won't come in. We told him his brother had

returned, but he only spat on the ground. He refuses to set foot in the house."

The father left the party and went to find the angry son. There were people coming and going, and in the twilight it was hard to recognize faces. Then he spotted him. "Please come in to the celebration, son," he said.

"I will not, Father," came the reply.

"Son, your brother is here, and he is alive and well. He is asking for you. Don't you want to see him?"

"Look. All this time I've been slaving for you and never disobeyed your orders. Yet you never even gave me a young goat so I could celebrate with my friends. But when this son who has squandered your property with prostitutes comes home, you kill a calf for him." The son looked at his father defiantly, knowing that every word was true and that every word would hurt. He wanted to hurt his father for the ignominy he felt inside.

The father looked his son in the eye. "My son, you are always with me and everything I have is yours. But we had to celebrate and be glad. Your brother was as dead, but now he is alive again; he was lost and is found."

This is all we have of the story. When I read the account of the prodigal son in Luke 15, I come smack against this ending. It causes me to wonder if the parchment the story was continued on got lost! I want to know how the older son reacted to his father's words. Did he defy his father and go off to have a little fun himself? Did he still refuse to join the party? Did he let bitterness rule the rest of his life? Or did he see his selfishness and share his father's rejoicing? We don't know. We are left hanging with the climax of the story untold.

Why was the parable cut short? I believe it's because we are told all that Jesus intended to teach us. The older son's reaction is not as critical as the father's confrontation. Jesus is painting a picture for Israel. There are lost sons of Israel whom God the Father wants in the kingdom. The older, established Jews wanted God's attention for themselves. Father-God (in Jesus) confronts His "older sons" with this thought: These lost ones aren't just My sons, they're also your brothers. In this confrontation between a joyous father and his oldest son, we witness the most sublime part of a father-son relationship—the confrontation.

Fathers who love their sons will stand in front of them and block their passage, not allowing them to walk unchallenged into danger.

Confrontation can be soft-spoken. It does not have to be angry. In essence, confrontation brings into the open all of the facts. A lawyer does this. He doesn't say things because he has a vendetta against the other side. In the same way, a father brings out the facts to establish a better way of living for his son and to encourage correct ways of thinking.

Confronters

I hate my car when it breaks down. Somehow, I feel violated and betrayed. Cars are made to run, and when they do not, I look upon them as useless. I'm not sure why I attach so much emotional energy to a broken-down car. Perhaps it's because it touches on two other emotional issues in my life: lost time and lost money.

The last time it quit functioning I was at my mom's house. We were planning to go to the beach that day. I loaded all the towels, bathing suits, lotion, flotation devices, reading material, lawn chairs, lunch, hats, sunglasses and beach balls into the trunk of the car. When I went to start it, it ran for a few seconds, rumbled an ominous roar and then stopped running.

After I had fumed for several minutes, my wife decided to spare my kids the benefits of watching my mindless tirade. She loaded the pile of paraphernalia into Mom's car, and they all went to the beach. All, that is, except me and my step-father Larry. He volunteered to walk with me to the service station where I was going to get the car fixed.

It was a long walk, and I spent the entire time waxing moronic about my "bucket of bolts." Finally, after 20 minutes of listening to me, Larry quietly said, "Mike, we could spend the day together fussing over your car. Or we could spend the time enjoying each other's company."

He spoke with great grace and love, but it was a confrontation. I'm sure over the years he has spent many, many hours rumbling and grumbling over the woes of vehicles. Now he was trying to spare me all that stomach acid. He also felt close enough to me to say something that would have been more painful coming from anyone else.

Fathers can get away with saying things that almost no one else can say. The relationship they maintain with their sons automatically carries the privilege and responsibility of being a confronter. If my mom had said the same thing, I would have ignored her, knowing she didn't understand cars or men.

Men, stand up tall. Confront your sons. That's an order!

Oh my son's my son,
till he gets him a wife,
But my daughter's my daughter
all of her life.

—Dinah Mulock Craik

Chapter 8

Sugar and Old Spice—
Fathers and Daughters

I can conjure up many wonderful images of my daughter. Our relationship is serene at this point (she is four years old). However, I have been warned that our lives may draw apart when the "Big P" begins to arrive. If I dwell on the thought, this "puberty monster" looms large and frightening.

But she is a long way from puberty at present, and we enjoy each other's company immensely. Every weekday morning I help my wife set out breakfast for our two school-age boys. Since Meaghan is not yet old enough for school, she is still a lady of leisure—she gets up when she wants to. However, Meaghan is also a morning person, and as soon as she is conscious that life is skipping by her, she jumps out of bed and starts what has become a daily routine for her and me.

I dress in sweats to go downstairs for calisthenics. She goes over to her tape recorder and puts on a praise and worship tape. I love exercise. She loves music. When my preliminary exercises are done, I enter our makeshift gymnasium: a sewing room with various weights, a cross-country ski trainer and a mini-trampoline. I set up the equipment, then put some worship music on my tape player. I have a good reason for doing this: The music draws my little girl.

As soon as she hears the music, she runs for the "gym." Together we do "the dance of joy," tickling each other, laughing and singing with the tape. Just the other day, we spent five wonderful minutes bouncing together on the trampoline. I held her small hands fatherly and firmly. She just smiled as the bouncing kept rhythm with "Let Your Spirit Rise within Me." The thought ran through my mind, *This is how a father and his daughter ought to relate. It can't be any better than this.*

Another kind of relationship

But later that morning in my office, while skimming a book, another thought came to me: *It's not that way for all fathers and daughters.*

Elizabeth Ward, an Australian creative writing teacher, has written a book called *Father-Daughter*

Rape. The *New Statesman Magazine* has called it "enormously valuable as the first major feminist study of incest." The reason I checked it out from the library was to examine exactly what people are saying about fathers and daughters.

I am not a stranger to child sexual abuse. For four years I was a founding director of a sexual abuse awareness group. In addition, I wrote an article for pastors explaining how they could be used to help victims of this horrible crime. In order to write that article, I examined much of the current literature on the subject. I had to wade through enormous amounts of commentary that owed more to Freud and Jung than it did to common sense. I became increasingly tired of being told that every relationship between a parent and child is tainted by some overwhelming sexual drive.

Yet I survived the plunge into this idiocy and gleaned some practical help as well as a clear understanding of how common incest is in the world. But in none of that reading did I come across anything as amazing as Elizabeth Ward's assessment of father-daughter rape.

Her first chapter begins with an analysis of Adam and Eve. Immediately, I stopped skimming and looked closely at her reasoning. Let me summarize her conclusion about the first couple.

1. Eve came out of Adam.
2. That makes Eve Adam's daughter.
3. God sanctioned their marriage.
4. God sanctioned the first case of incest.

Ludicrous you say? That's not all.

1. God called Eve His daughter and Adam His son.
2. They had one Father.
3. Therefore, they were brother and sister.
4. Therefore, God sanctioned the first brother-sister incest.
5. Eve, as temptress, initiates this incestuous bond.

Ward then concludes, "Father-daughter sexual union is implicitly sanctioned, from the Bible to the latest movie star marriage." Fathers everywhere who do not commit incest with their daughters are being accused by various branches of psychology as wishing they could. What is implicitly implied from Freud to Ward is that there is no affection and bonding between a father and a daughter that is divorced from sexual desire. Those conclusions make me physically ill.

The idea that God's Word would ever sanction sin is impossible. The crime is that father-daughter rape is happening. It is occurring where I live, and it is occurring where you live.

One out of four girls will be sexually abused before she reaches 18. And the majority of these abusers will be their own fathers.

But biology is not destiny. There is a brigade of dads on the sidelines of their daughters' lives, cheering their every exploit, hugging their sadness away, wearing a silly grin at their awards day at preschool, graduation and wedding. We are not ugly brutes who have evil in our hearts. There truly is a caucus of concerned fathers who have committed their daughters to God and would not harm them in any way.

The Bible, of course, does not advocate abusing children—or anyone for that matter. In fact, it is the greatest guidebook on women's liberation. Elizabeth Ward espouses the ideal of feminism—the liberation of all women, young and old, from the tyranny of men. Yet what feminism has not yet understood how to accomplish, God has already done.

From Eve to Mary, from Ruth to Martha, there is a consistent pattern of behavior exemplified by Father-God toward His daughters. In saying this, I want to reemphasize that certain actions of God pertain equally to men and women. He forgives us all. He forms a relationship forever with us all. He sets us all free from sin. He heals men and women with equal willingness. He gives both men and women His Holy Spirit, and all the gifts of the Spirit are available to both His sons and daughters. But Father-God handles His daughters differently than He does His sons. Surprisingly, at the core of God's dealings with His daughters is the same motivation that fuels the feminist movement: liberation.

God wants to liberate women. He has set a course for them that diverges from the one He sets for men. Let's look at what He says about how fathers should treat their daughters.

Liberation from sin's effects

Teams of artists and specialized restoration experts are finally coming to the end of the cleaning of the Sistine Chapel, where artist Michelangelo's famous paintings cover the walls and ceilings. Great pains have been taken as every minute particle of grime was removed from the murals. Now that the original colors are showing through, a new conclusion is being made about their creator.

Michelangelo was a different kind of painter than anyone thought he was. For centuries, the Italian master had been viewed as a somber, morose fellow. Most of this evaluation was based on the biblical scenes he painted for the chapel. The colors were muted and the details appeared fuzzy, as if the artist was painting a dream, not an authentic vision.

But the renewed paintings have changed the experts' minds. Centuries of smoke and wax had caked over the paint, obscuring the real art and the real artist. In actuality, the original colors are bold and believable, lifelike and entirely haunting. When I noticed the before and after pictures, the difference was phenomenal. The details and hue are distinct and flavorful, revealing a mind that was keen and full of vigor. No one could look at the Sistine Chapel now and call Michelangelo morose!

In the same way, it is important for fathers to liberate their daughters from the smoke screen of sin. A baby girl is born in sin, which simply means that she is the offspring of sinners and that every chromosome contains the cumulative effects of hundreds of generations of sin. A young girl who has not even understood what sin against a holy God is will instinctively enter into sinful behavior and be effected by the results of sin all around her.

When Adam and Eve entered into sin, the world changed, and they changed forever. This first family experienced the callousness of sin's clutches and recoiled with horror as they considered the prospects of paradise lost.

In other words, they were not happy with what their sin had brought them. We have already examined what sin did to Adam and every son after him. But what did sin do to Eve and her daughters?

Genesis 3:16 capsulizes the changes that were about to occur in Eve's life: "I will greatly increase your pains in childbearing;/ with pain you will give birth to children./ Your desire will be for your husband, / and he will rule over you."

If you compare what God said after that to Adam with what He says to Eve, there is one startling difference: Adam's challenges related to the environment and workplaces that would surround him. Eve's challenges are centered on two different relationships—children and husband.

Some scholars have questioned the phrase "greatly increase your pains," because it seems to imply a prior point of reference. How do you increase something that has never happened? If you give your child an allowance, increasing it will increase his joy. If that same child has never received an allowance, the promise of an increase may produce confused looks.

The only explanation that makes sense in this "increase of pains" matter is that God had already explained to Eve what the birth procedure would entail. Perhaps she had observed animals giving birth and had asked God about it. We can only assume that God had it in mind to minimize the pain and effort of giving birth to and nurturing children.

But sin increases pain. That is a universal law that applies to us. Pain, however, is not a punishment. Judgment for sin comes after we die. Pain is the challenge that exists when sin enters our lives. Eve's pain would be mixed with life's most joyous occasion. Her torturous experience would result in life, which, in essence, is a gift from God. These pains are not punishments; they are intrinsic challenges to be overcome in the seeking of God's glory.

First male-female relationship

The second change in Eve's life would be her relationship to Adam. She will desire and cling to her husband in dependence. As a result of this, he will be placed in a position of rulership over his wife. Headship existed before the Fall because God made Adam the primary head of the human race. But only in the Fall does *headship* broaden its base into *rulership*. Sin's effects in a hostile world will bring fear into Eve's heart and cause her to desire Adam's care and protection.

Of course, she would desire more than just protection. Whereas Adam will find his fulfillment in the work of his hands, Eve will be satisfied when her family relationships are secure and growing. As much as this flies in the face of modern thought, no one has been able to explain why women are relationship-oriented and men are task-oriented. Sin did not do this; it only highlighted gender differences.

A young girl's first male-female relationship is with her father. In a relationship sense, Dad becomes the lord to whom his daughter is drawn. Nurturing children can be taught with dolls and later with younger siblings. But where does a little girl learn how to relate to men? From the place that should be safest—Dad.

In 1987, Erma Bombeck wrote a Father's Day column that made a lasting impression on me. She describes her ambivalent ideas about her father in this way:

> My dad left the house every morning and always seemed glad to see everyone at night.
>
> He opened the jar of pickles when no one else could.
>
> He was the only one in the house who wasn't afraid to go into the basement by himself.
>
> He cut himself shaving but no one kissed it or got excited about it.
>
> He signed all my report cards. He put me to bed early. He took lots of pictures, but was

never in them.

I was afraid of everyone else's father, but not my own. Once I made him tea. It was only sugar water, but he sat on a small chair and said it was delicious. He looked very uncomfortable.

Whenever I played house, the mother doll had a lot to do. I never knew what to do with the daddy doll, so I had him say, "I'm going off to work now" and threw him under the bed.

When I was nine years old, my father didn't get up one morning and go to work. He went to the hospital and died the next day.

I went to my room and felt under the bed for the father doll. When I found him, I dusted him off and put him on my bed.

He never did anything. I didn't know his leaving would hurt so much.

I still don't know why.

That column is the still-life photo of so many grown women who were unknowingly cut out of their father's lives. Not long ago, I prayed with a woman who was having trouble trusting her husband. Yet in every way she painted him as the glowing leader of the household. "Has he ever let you down?" I asked. Tears ran down her face as she noiselessly shook her head. This man had never let her down. "But I know he will," she concluded.

Then we talked about her father. He was not present during her growing-up years. To the little girl who sat before me in a grown woman's body, Daddy was still gone. Only now the first lord of her life is replaced with another lord. This second lord is required to be two men—husband and Daddy. Because he was not fulfilling the other, he summarily failed at both.

This counseling scenario is more common with women than any other dilemma. They miss their fathers, and they can never get them back.

Fathers who refuse to take the time to get to know their daughters are abandoning them just as if they physically left. Remember, God determined that there would be an innate female desire for a male-female relationship. Many girls who find themselves bereft of this relationship with Dad will settle for any relationship with any boy who will give them the affection and closeness they crave. I am not saying that women cannot survive without a father's love. For many girls who have suffered fatherly abandonment, Father-God offers His closeness. But for dads who read these words—let's fulfill the role God gives us as the man in our daughters' lives. Let's be the lord they need.

Liberation from stereotypes

In the early '70s a rock group called The Five-Man Electric Band recorded a hit song, "Signs." In a way it is a disjointed group of verses connected by different signs that the songwriter had read. I still remember one verse of the song, even though I haven't heard it for years. That verse spoke of stereotypes:

> The sign said, "Long-haired freaky people need not apply!"
>
> So I tucked my hair up under my hat, and I went in to ask him why.
>
> He said, "You look like a fine, upstanding young man. I think you'll do."
>
> So I took off my hat
> and said, "Imagine that,
> huh, me workin' for you?"

The song is lamenting the stereotype that says there is an inverse relationship between hair length and the quality of work done. The longer the hair, the less competent the man must be. That is a stereotype. It is a judgment on what a person is, based on one or more external qualifications. Usually, there is some history behind most stereotypes. The problem exists when someone else's actions and failures dictate how everyone feels about you, a member of a stereotypical group.

I performed the wedding of a church member who had, just prior to the nuptials, become a Christian. The great majority of the wedding guests were unsaved and unhomogenized with my view on life. The reception was, to say the least, an education in how people view God and pastors. One brief conversation says enough.

"So you're a preacher, huh? What church?"

"Uh . . . the Alliance church," I answered, hoping I wouldn't have to explain the longer name, The Christian and Missionary Alliance—a living monument to accuracy tied with a tongue twister.

"Never heard of it. What are you like?"

"Well, somewhere between Baptist and Pentecostal," I reasoned, hoping that this found a point of reference with my questioner.

"So you're one of those hell-'n-brimstone preachers. Hey guys, this here's a hell-'n-brimstone preacher. Who wants a sermon?"

And so on.

All of us hate being stereotyped. Perhaps this explains, in part, the proliferation of women working outside the home. Seemingly forever, women have been locked into a cage whose bars resemble the words, "A woman's place is in the home." In case that particular encasement were not restrictive enough, some men have narrowed it down further: "A woman's place is in the kitchen." Others have modified this by adding other conditions such as "barefoot and pregnant." Sounds like a *great* job description. No wonder so many women are bailing out of this stereotype.

Today's culture did not invent female stereotyping. In Bible times it flourished. The Jews tended to view women as only the barest step above Gentile dogs. Greek men held similar views of women. They locked their wives in the house and forbade them from ever leaving as long as they were married. Women found outside of their homes were often considered cult prostitutes and were treated as such.

The best thing
Jesus, the Father's complete representation on

earth, shows all men how to break apart silly stereotypes. Fathers everywhere ought to separate their daughters from the confines of this bondage just as Jesus did for two of His favorite women: Mary and Martha.

The now famous account of Mary and Martha is found in Luke 10:38–42. Jesus and His disciples stopped in a village called Bethany, and Martha opened her home to them. As the Master and His group relaxed, He took advantage of the time to teach the disciples, who had recently returned from a missionary journey. Mary, Martha's sister, was so enthralled with Jesus' words that she sat intently at His feet listening. Martha, meanwhile, slaved over a hot stove in the kitchen.

Before long, Martha came into the room where Jesus was speaking. Exasperated (and probably a little jealous), she said to Jesus, "Lord, don't you care that my sister has left me to do the work by myself? Tell her to help me!"

Every eye turned to Mary. Murmurs of agreement swept the crowd gathered in Martha's home. No doubt several of the men had wanted to echo the same sentiment as they observed her take the closest seat in the most audacious way. After all, Mary *was* a woman, and this was really a *man's* scene. Martha, in her frustration, was putting into words what men all over the room were feeling. They waited for the Master's reaction. Would He allow injustice to continue?

"Martha, Martha," He said. He looked at her with kindness in His eyes. He knew her hard work, her steadfast and loyal servanthood. In essence, she was the church of Ephesus personified. But He wanted something else from her.

"You are worried and upset about many things, but only one thing is needed. Mary has chosen what is better, and it will not be taken away from her." Jesus declared Mary free to sit among the men at His feet.

Liberation. With these words, Jesus declared all women free to be themselves. They were free to sit at His feet for a while instead of always being men's servants. They were free to express themselves with the inner beauty God crafted them with. They were liberated to be unique servants in God's plan, unshackled by stereotypical expectations.

Consider Margaret Thatcher, the former "Iron Lady" of British politics. Her bold and stoic approach to life would never have been possible without a father and, later, a husband who liberated her.

On the day she first moved into Number 10 Downing Street as prime minister, she gave homage to her father: "He brought me up to believe all the things I do believe, and they're the values on which I have fought the election. It's passionately interesting to me that the things I learned in a small town, in a very modest home, are just the things that I believe have won the election. I owe almost everything to my father."

Notice what is "passionately interesting" to Thatcher—that her beliefs, values and winning thoughts were based on what was passed down to her by *her father*! Somehow, this man of vision was freed from seeing his girl as a housekeeper-in-training. I can imagine he passed down his view on life in fireside chats, in books explaining the "hows" and "whys" of life and in an attitude of complete acceptance for whatever his "Maggie" would become. If she had become a seamstress or a superstar, it would have been the same, as long as she maximized the grand potential within her.

My daughter Meaghan and I share a love for musical worship. We dance together, sing together and love the same worship tapes. My sons like music but not nearly as much as Meaghan does.

When I play the guitar, she always comes to hear, even when her "cool" brothers are too busy for such things. I want my daughter to be the greatest servant in God's hands that she can be. I want to teach her what I am also giving to my sons—the desire to be all God wants her to be. I put no restrictions on Meaghan that I do not put also on my sons.

In short, I am not raising Meaghan to *be* something. I am raising her to *have* something—my every idea and focus that I can give her. I yearn to release her to be a Deborah or a Ruth—whomever God decides.

A father can set the tone for his daughter's life. As he accepts her ideas, swoons over her accomplishments and pushes her to be all she can be, she will begin to accept the idea that she can be anything. Then, if a father encourages his daughter to sit at the feet of Jesus, she will find herself listening to the One who can liberate her from the inner stereotypes of sin—something a father really can't touch. When she has heard from her Heavenly Father, her heart will become steadfast and immovable.

Some may suppose that I am advocating raising a woman to act as a man. In order to believe this, one would have to conclude that certain services rendered to God are decidedly male and others expressly female. I have no quarrel with those who believe this, though I cannot fully share the idea. Let me explain why.

Service to God, done properly, is rendered to God alone. True service does not mind if those we serve on earth smell nice or salivate on our sleeve. It is all the same—service to God. Brother Lawrence, in his devotional book *Practicing the Presence of God*, saw the washing of dishes as service to God. He did it for God's sake, not for the sake of his own ego or for the sake of the monastery. Every soap bubble popped its praise to God when it was lathered by his worshipful hands.

My point is this: What a woman renders to God in humility and obedience is service to God. As a father to my little girl, I want her to be released from seeing only certain things as her way to serve God. I yearn for her to be anything God wants her to be.

Love first; rules second

The calendar hanging in Meaghan's room is filled with warm images of little girls. Last January, my wife, Kathy, urged me to flip over a page to February. As a calendar purist, I usually like to be surprised by next month's offering—but only when it was the first of the month.

This time I cheated. I'm glad I did.

The photo was of an angelic girl perched on a big piano bench. She strained to reach the keys, but she looked like a great maestro working at her craft. Kathy and I both touched Meaghan who was standing between us.

Lately, she has been sitting at the bench of our newly acquired piano. She plays diligently, one note at a time. She lacks rhythm, tempo, chording, structure, voice and counterpoint. In short, she makes nothing but noise.

Sometimes I find myself wishing she would stop the banging. But a friend of ours who teaches music told us to be glad. "She obviously loves the piano," the woman said. "Don't discourage her. In time she'll come to see that certain uses of the piano work out better than others. Then she can learn the rules." So we're letting her love the piano first; then, later, she can learn the rules.

Mary knew that principle. She desired to love the Master first, then she would obey Him in whatever service He suggested. A good father will not limit his daughter. Let God set the limits by His Word and Spirit.

Liberation from sexual pitfalls

The rumor was traveling rapidly through the church. One of the leaders in the church youth group, a prize pupil, a supposed paragon of Christian parents and Christian schools, was pregnant at 16 years of age. How everyone found out so quickly is anyone's guess. People were shocked. They could not imagine how such a fine teen could get into that kind of trouble.

I know how she did it. This is the '90s. These kinds of errors have become commonplace. Sure, her upbringing was supposed to inoculate her against the disease of fornication. But the blatantly obvious fact that it had not was the knife that scarred the sensibilities of those who knew her family.

The girl telephoned my wife one afternoon to let her know of the situation—"before anyone else tells you," as she put it. My wife could not tell her we already knew, just as she could not tell her that everything would work out all right. We knew in our hearts that this girl faced a future of uncertainty and doubts. Though we could help soften those blows through love and acceptance, the stained reputation and ruined plans would not go away.

Over the months, as the baby grew, we had many times to talk with our pregnant young friend. She became closer and closer to my wife and me. It was as if she had discovered a new comfort zone— people who still accepted her as she was.

One of our conversations stands out from the rest. We had been laughing together most of the evening, when she began to cry. I asked her what was wrong.

"My father really hates me now," she said. "Before, he barely tolerated me. But now he hates me!" Her sobs were laced with bitterness.

I knew her father well. Before this incident occurred, he constantly bragged about his daughter. "What makes you think he hates you?" I asked.

"Look at me! Do I look like a dream daughter to you?"

"But he's always been proud of you," I told her. "There are many times he has told me and others about your accomplishments."

"If he's so proud of me, then why did he stop touching me?" she asked.

I had no idea what she was talking about, so I asked. "What are you referring to?"

She hesitated and wiped back the tears. "Three years ago he took me out for dinner, and we were having a great time. Then out of the blue he told me that he couldn't hug me anymore. That was the reason we had gone out for dinner—just to tell me *that*!"

"Did he ever tell you why?" I asked.

"All he said was that he didn't think it would be right, whatever that means. Pastor, how can it be wrong for a dad to hug his daughter?" Then she broke down completely, folding herself into a fetal position, while Kathy cradled her.

Two things became obvious to me. On one hand, here was a father who, in the emergence of his daughter's puberty, had warded off his insecurities by cutting off his affection for her. On the other hand, here was a girl entering the great biological, emotional and relational changes of puberty. When affection was not forthcoming from Dad, she desired someone else to give it to her. That someone else (or, as we learned, several "someone elses") taught her sexual behavior—but he did not satisfy her desire to be accepted and shown affection by her dad.

First sweetheart

Dad is a girl's first sweetheart. When she finds a lifelong companion and guide in her father, then she will be much more choosy in dating and courtship. Therefore, Dad's affection must be an ever-flowing stream—dramatic and fast-flowing at some points, slow and predictable at other places.

It is *not* Dad's job to replace boyfriends. I think of a McDonald's restaurant commercial I saw some time ago. Dad picks up his girl at school, and they spend a warm and special time together. Emotion and affection join each other in a cavalcade of family love. Later on, Dad drives his girl and her friends to McDonald's. When she leaves the car to go inside, he gets out to go with her. She looks at him with horror, "You're not going, too, are you?" Then Dad spots some boys in the restaurant. He quickly gets back in to the car, mumbling some excuses.

No, dads are not given the responsibility of cloistering their fair maidens in the closet until they're 30 years old. Our role is to be the first man and the ideal man in a young girl's life. There is no greater role in the universe for a father to play. In this role, he is the one who holds and comforts and challenges. Because his role is not sexual, he is able to teach all these elements of a male-female relationship that come before and after sex. In short, Dad shows his little girl how she ought to be treated—and how to treat men.

American poet Ogden Nash, writing to his daughter who was considering leaving her husband for a much older man, said this:

> It bothers me to think you have sloppy—not sophisticated, but sloppy—ideas about life. I have never tried to blind you to any side of life, through any form of censorship, trusting in your intelligence to learn of, and to recognize evil without approving or participating in it. . . . Just keep yourself in hand and remember that generally speaking it's better to call older men, Mister.
> I love you tremendously,
> Daddy.

There was a dad who continued to play his role with great heart.

What can a father teach?

The Bible also tells us how God treated a daughter of pubescent age and virginal experience. The young woman was Mary, the mother of Jesus.

We read in Luke 1:28 that "The angel went to [Mary] and said, 'Greetings, you who are highly favored! The Lord is with you.'" When you consider all that was about to happen, this does not sound like enough of an explanation of how God felt about Mary. But when you consider how Mary must have received this, it gives us a great deal of insight into what God was doing for her.

First, God was not required to communicate what was going to happen. God can do anything He wants. She would have found out about the baby soon enough. Why bother saying anything?

As a girl enters puberty and begins menstruating, there is great fear and curiosity. Fathers sometimes let their wives do all the explaining concerning this time of life. For some of this schooling, a mother is a much more capable teacher. A father has never had a monthly period. A father has never known female bodily changes.

So what can the father teach? Acceptance and knowledge of the future. In sending Gabriel, God let Mary know that He was going to be with her through the struggles of the forthcoming pregnancy. He would not reject her, even though others would write her off as a fallen woman.

Getting back to the story above about the pregnant teen at our church—I spent some time with her father after discovering where the source of her ache lay. I brought what she had told me to his attention, while telling him that I understood how he must have felt.

He was stunned. He literally collapsed back in his chair as the weight of his seemingly innocuous actions caught up with his understanding. Then he began to cry—sounding much as his daughter had when she broke down in our family room—remorseful and bitter.

"Mike, what can I do now?" he asked. "She's already pregnant."

"You can do now what you could have done before. Pour out your love on her. Show her you care. Don't shove her even farther away just because you are embarrassed by the results."

He followed my counsel and began to show his daughter how much he cared for her. At first, it was hard for both of them to accept. But as it got easier, a distinct change was visible. At church, their hands would be locked together as Frank introduced her to new people.

They've both got some tough years ahead. But they can make it if they don't draw apart from one another.

Gabriel, on behalf of God, said, "The Lord is with you." What a marvelous invitation to Mary. Now, in the age of the Holy Spirit, we take for granted that God is always with us, that He will never leave us nor forsake us. But in Mary's world, God's presence came in the form of a cloud, or pillar of fire, or the Shekinah Glory. But the angel is sent to give her this message: "I'm with you all the way, My daughter."

There is no better way of preparing a young woman for a world of potential sexual relationships, than by creating a cocoon of comfort where she always feels assured of Daddy's love.

Notice, also, Mary's reaction to her Heavenly Father,

My soul glorifies the Lord
    and my spirit rejoices in God my Savior,
    for he has been mindful
      of the humble state of his servant.
From now on all generations will call me
    blessed,
    for the Mighty One has done great things
    for me—
    holy is his name. (Luke 1:46–49)

Mary's pregnancy brought her joy. Her Father accepted her and sent His love in a way she could understand. A father's daughter understands the pitfalls of sex when she understands that he will always love and cherish her.

It is easier for the generous to forgive than for the offender to ask forgiveness.
—James Tomson

Forgive many things in others: nothing in yourself.
—Decimus Ausonius

Chapter 9

The Final Frontier— Fathers and Forgiveness

I was getting ready to dicker over the price of a bronze elephant when the kiosk owner rudely pulled the item out of my hand. He kicked down the pole that supported the awning and folded up his shop, wares and all, locking them tight with a padlock before racing down the street. All of this took 10 seconds.

That's when I noticed the crowd pushing past me. It was not as if they were all running. In that case I would have looked around for Godzilla, or in this scene, a ravaging lion. But the African market I had chosen to shop in that day was flowing, gliding as an elixir of liquid people, pulling others along in a type of psychological cohesion. Where were they all going? The babel-like chorus of voices didn't help me, for I couldn't speak Bambara. I turned to my missionary friend who was as startled as I was.

"Jeanne, what's happening? What's going on?"

"I haven't a clue," she responded. She looked genuinely puzzled. For a moment we stood together motionless, feeling much as boulders in a fast-moving stream.

"Let's go find John," she finally concluded. "He'll know what's happening."

We found Jeanne's husband on the boardwalk where the dried fish were being displayed and sold. He motioned for us to join him at a booth. He was talking to an Arabic-looking man.

"Court is in session, Mike," he said to my query of what was going on. "Mohammed here says that if we go over to the ravine, we'll witness the West African judicial system. He seems quite eager for us to follow him."

So off we went. The crowd was now flowing with us, and inexorably, we were led to the place where the drama was unfolding. It was a place we had crossed over when we drove to the market. It was an overgrown gully, which only filled with water when the rains came. This was a Sahel drought year, and thus the floodway was bone-dry. But it certainly was not empty—not today!

John pieced together the story from the turbulent Tourareg crowd pressed in around us. Someone had stolen a gold locket from a merchant in the main square. In his flight he sought to hide in the bulrushes and thorn bushes of the floodway. If it were only a half-dozen posse members looking for him in the dense underbrush, he would probably have escaped detection. But this was West Africa; thievery is punished by the whole community!

Hundreds of men with thick canes descended into the ravine, beating a path before them. The crowd above hummed a threatening chorus. This lasted for several minutes. Then I heard a different sound: a solitary voice raised up in high-pitched agony.

The thief had been found, and his lips uttered a cry of pain inflicted upon him by those dealing out harsh justice. This man would never steal again— nor would he do anything again. He had exchanged his life for a gold piece. My missionary comrades just shook their heads as we walked away from this cruel display of justice.

"WAWA," John said. Jeanne nodded in reluctant agreement as we walked. I was too stunned at that moment to ask what the word meant. But later, after many more surprises, the meaning came home clearly: West Africa Wins Again.

Practicing forgiveness

Many in our Western culture express outrage at any form of punitive justice. They push for rehabilitation, as if there existed an ideal plane upon which this justice could be meted out. Their ideal assumes goodness and equity in the judicial system. It also assumes that mankind has the ability aside from God's help to better itself. Of course, all of these assumptions are not biblically substantiated.

Men will sin. Some sins will primarily offend God alone. Others will offend other individuals and God. Still other sins will offend the community at large, breaking laws that reflect a sense of community respect for a consensus of morality. In the United States, the Bible has long been recognized as the source of this moral consensus. Even though this ideal is decaying, no other moral system has arisen with the power to usurp the Bible's place.

The Bible gives authority to the state to mete out justice. Individuals may not exact justice. We are not allowed to repay evil for evil. But the state may punish sin. It is not, however, in the state's best interests to practice forgiveness. That is a system that steps beyond justice. A state is fortunate if its actions are just. Mercy belongs in the hands of a different Authority.

God forgives. The Church is called to forgive. So must the family learn to forgive. And because the father stands as the legal representative of a nuclear family, he must bear responsibility for the existence and practice of forgiveness in his family.

The parable of the prodigal son enlarges our view of the forgiving nature of Father-God. Because it does that, it is an example of forgiveness in the family setting. The father of this story is the central figure; it is his unusual action that transforms the scene from mundane tragedy to high and holy drama. It rightly could be titled "The Parable of the Forgiving Father."

One large role the Christian father must play is that of the forgiver. This role has the capability of being the most frustrating of all the parts the father must attempt to act out. But as we will observe, fatherly forgiveness is a key to letting kingdom life flow in the current of a family's relationship to God.

A father's role is to back away

The tendency to view the parable through the experiences of the profligate son and not through the long-suffering father is actually an error caused by not considering the context of the chapter in which the story is found. The parable of the forgiving father is the third and final parable in a series of teachings on lost things. Luke 15 records stories about a lost sheep and a lost coin—and one about a lost son.

But the point of each is not that the sheep, coin and son were lost. Rather it is found in *the effort expended to retrieve what was lost*. In the parable of the lost sheep, the shepherd goes out and finds it and brings it in, capping the rescue mission with a grand party. In the next, a woman loses a silver coin and tears her house apart looking for it. When it is located, she throws a party.

The last parable has one notable difference from the others: the father does not go out searching for his son. Luke 15:11–16 tells us,

There was a man who had two sons. The younger one said to his father, "Father, give me my share of the estate." So he divided his property between them.

Not long after that, the younger son got together all he had, set off for a distant country and there squandered his wealth in wild living. After he had spent everything, there was a severe famine in that whole country, and he began to be in need. So he went and hired himself out to a citizen of that country, who sent him to his fields to feed pigs. He longed to fill his stomach with the pods that the pigs were eating, but no one gave him anything.

Understand the lessons of this story. The father does nothing to stop his young son from destroying his future. He does not refuse his son's request for funds. He does not lecture his boy incessantly on the dangers of wine, women and wild living. He doesn't send a note to this guy's youth pastor telling him to do a Bible study series on "Obeying Your Parents"! This father, who we can assume is a type of our Heavenly Father, is particularly noteworthy for doing absolutely nothing to stop his hell-bent son.

Most of us have seen the bumper sticker gracing the back of a $50,000 Winnebego that says, "We're spending our kids' inheritance." In our affluent modern society, it is not necessary for parents to pass their estate to their children. But in Jesus' day, a son might end up destitute unless he were given a portion of his father's possessions. Back then, millions of man-hours went into the construction of a family fortune. It was to be cherished and anticipated. An inheritance of any note was as good an assurance of affluence in old age as anyone had then.

But this boy ground the inheritance under his heel. He wanted his portion immediately, and he wanted it for *himself*. He had no thought past the fun and frolicking that beckoned him from distant lands. Verse 13 says the son "got together all he had." How do you gather an inheritance? You turn your assets into cash by selling them. He traded in his future—his lands, his livestock, his whole being—for good hard cash.

Then he set out for anywhere but where Dad lived. From the sounds of his lifestyle, he hooked up with the ancient equivalent of Las Vegas. His cash flowed faster, and his inheritance shrunk quicker than he ever could have imagined.

Why didn't his father warn him before he left?

We don't know what was said when the boy left. Maybe Dad gave him sage advice. But the Scripture recounts to us the most critical teaching point: He gave his son the inheritance, even though he probably knew what his son was going to do with it.

"We'll be praying for you"

In the years we have to influence our children, we see a thousand serpents in the grass. We run out with our verbal machetes hoping to make the way smoother for them. Fathers who discipline their kids do so with the hope that it will produce character and common sense.

I remember the evening when one of our elders called me in a panic. In a few tense minutes he explained how his son was throwing away his whole life by asking some girl (he spat out the word "girl") to marry him. The boy was 19 and a brilliant student. The girl in question appeared to many in the church to be slightly less than intelligent and certainly unsuited for the young man she was dating. Dad wanted me to talk them out of marriage. How could his son ever go to medical school with a wife like that attached to him?

I agreed to see them. In my heart I also knew they were making a mistake. The girl was a loose-living, nominal believer, and as I found out in our talk, the son was dating her because of the sexual relationship they were having. He enjoyed it. He also resented everyone telling him how wrong it all was.

I told them I thought they were too young, that their sexual relationship was wrong. I told them the marriage was a bad idea.

They told me to take a hike. They told Mom and Dad the same thing in slightly different words.

That's when Dad did something I will admire forever. He shook his son's hand and said, "We'll be praying for you son, and we hope you have a good marriage. Remember always that Mom and I love you." Later, he confessed that he could have never uttered those words if the Holy Spirit had not controlled him.

This is the message of the parable. A father must sense when rebellion is too far-blown to be contained. Of course, I do not refer to the rebellion of young children. But as children grow into puberty, there are many occasions when their decisions are resolute, and they fly in the face of our wishes. At that point it is biblically wise to wish them well, shed a few tears and leave the door open for when they may come back.

I am not referring to the child who wants to live like a hellion *and* enjoy home's comforts. There ought to be rules in a home that are inviolate. But when the child wants to make a decision that will affect him more than anyone else, it is time to say what wisdom would do, then back off.

The living of that child's life is no longer our concern. We created him, but he is uniquely distinct from us.

Jesus, in telling this parable, paints the landscape of the Father's emotions as He views His created beings annihilating their lives through countless idiotic decisions. Yet God does not close the door on any of us or tell us not to come back.

A friend of mine, Tim, works for the Youth With A Mission headquarters in Montana. He told me a story from one of his missionary journeys that exemplifies this principle. His singing group was in Portland, Oregon, holding concerts and preaching the gospel among the street people of that city. After one concert, a young man approached, wearing a bedraggled look and an arrogant chip on his shoulder.

"How can you preach to us?" he began. "You don't know anything about us. You've never lived on the streets. You've never slept in a box. I'd like to see you try it, preacher, and then talk about the love of God."

So Tim did! He moved onto the streets with another member of the team. The two of them tagged along with the man who had issued the challenge. They learned to live by panhandling. They suffered the degradation of being part of life's human refuse. They endured the stares of pious passersby whose looks were accusing and unnerving. But they also continued to talk about Jesus' love and to read from the Word to their friend.

Little by little, the ministry of reconciliation began to work. As the love of God softened the heart of this street-toughened 25-year-old, he began to ask deeper, more penetrating questions. The two missionaries answered the ones they could. At one point, the conversation stopped. The man's eyes glossed over with tears.

"I've gotta call home," he blurted out. Then he raced down the street to a public telephone. He spoke in animated fashion as Tim looked on. Then he handed the phone to Tim.

"My dad wants to talk to you" was all he said.

"Hello," Tim said haltingly.

The other end of the phone crackled. Then a man's voice came on. He was hoarse from crying, but he told Tim his story. The father on the other end was an evangelist. His son had left home several years before to live his own life. They had prayed for him continually, but had never heard from him—until now.

"Tim, I want to tell you something. . . . Thank you . . . " He couldn't go on. He sobbed tears of joy over the phone. Then the line went dead.

For forgiveness to be the rule of thumb in family life, a father must never close permanently the doors of communication. In acknowledging that we cannot control our children's lives, we as fathers must also decide that their dumb decisions can never cause us to cut them off.

A father's role is to bestow forgiveness

One of the "sayings on the cross" relates to this issue of forgiveness. Luke 23:34 reads: "Jesus said, 'Father, forgive them, for they do not know what they are doing.' " Because Jesus always prayed according to the Father's will, He must have known this was the overwhelming desire of our Heavenly Father. Jesus didn't die on the cross to twist Father-God's arm so hard that He would have to forgive us. Father-God was the One who sent Jesus. It was the Father's business that Jesus was doing. Forgiveness is in the realm of, and in the hands of, the Father.

It may be said also in the much more limited confines of family life that it is the prerogative of the father to bring forgiveness to his children. Or at the very least, we may say that it is the father's office to seek forgiveness for his children.

Job clearly exemplifies this ministry. In Job 1:4–5 we read about this.

> His sons used to take turns holding feasts in their homes, and they would invite their three sisters to eat and drink with them. When a period of feasting had run its course, Job would send and have them purified. Early in the morning he would sacrifice an offering for each one of them, thinking, "Perhaps my children have sinned and cursed God in their hearts." This was Job's regular custom.

Job was concerned that his children be right with God. With that example, he shows all fathers that the ministry of forgiveness is upon the father as leader and priest in his house.

In Luke 15 we return to the boy who had absconded with his early inheritance. When hard times hit and all his good-time-Charlie friends said, "Adios," he got hit with a dilemma. Famine was everywhere. No one feeds a stranger when they can't feed their own families. The only job around was found in a local farmer's pig sty.

Think of it: a Jewish boy having to touch and care for pigs. How ignominious! How far this lad had come from the palatial life he used to enjoy in his father's home. Hard times and hard-to-swallow grub have a way of bringing a man to his senses.

The pods he drooled over were not pea pods. At least those would have been edible. These were carob pods that normally were used to feed livestock and sometimes were chopped up to make a poor man's vegetable. They were sour and not good food. Verse 16 makes it clear in the original language that he was yearning to eat from the pile the pigs had already been eating from. No self-respecting Jew would ever think of eating from a place where pigs had been—let alone eating the food they were eating.

He must have been extremely hungry. But, adding insult to ignominy, his boss wouldn't even let him eat carob pods. That's when the beginnings of repentance stirred the cockles of his heart. The wheels began to turn as he considered what his father's slaves were eating. It far outdistanced the slop he was shoveling. So a plan began to form in his mind.

I'll say this, he thought. *Father, I have sinned against heaven and you. I am no longer worthy to be called your son. Make me one of your day laborers.* Whether he meant the words or not is impossible to tell. But that is not the point. Any sane human being would have thought the same thing had hunger twisted his stomach into an organic pretzel.

The key to this story, as I have already mentioned, is the father's reaction when the boy returned home with his precalculated repentance. In the original language we can find some subtle insight into how the father was feeling toward his lost son. Verse 20 says that the father saw his son "while he was still a long way off." The Greek word used here to designate the great distance is a word we have taken into the English language—*macro*. The son was macro-miles away—and yet his father spotted him! We can assume that the father had good eyesight—and that he was determined to be the first person to spot the fledgling if he ever returned to the nest.

I can envision the father making this a daily ritual. Every morning as he went to the fields, he peered intently down the dusty road. Long minutes he would stand in that reflective pose. Then again, as his day's work was done, he might give the road a final parting stare, just to close that day properly.

Then one day he spotted someone on the road. His son was coming toward him, and the particles of dust he kicked up were like granules of gold to the joyous father. The boy's head may have been bowed in shame. But Dad's head was up, waiting for the moment his boy would return.

The next few words express even more of the father's heart: He was "filled with compassion for him" (verse 20). His emotional being went into a tizzy. Then "he ran to his son." In his popular Christian song, Benny Hester puts this story in a unique perspective—"It was the only time I ever saw God run . . . when He ran to me!" The father had waited long for this day.

Then we are told that the father "threw his arms around him and kissed him."

Missing corn chips!

We represent heaven to our children. Before they come to recognize, worship and serve their

Heavenly Father, they run face-to-face with their earthly father. Many times that confrontation will either aid or scar a child's opinion of God. An abusive father will conjure the image of a perpetually punishing and quasi-vindictive, unfair God. An absent father will evoke questions about the existence of Father-God. A merciful, loving, forgiving father, who is also capable of punishing, will develop the concept, slowly but distinctly, that Father-God is merciful, loving, forgiving and capable of disciplining His children.

One of the keys of the kingdom as outlined in the Gospels is the right to pronounce and bestow forgiveness on another person. John 20:23 says, "If you forgive anyone his sins, they are forgiven." This key is especially helpful to a father's career as heavenly representative. The prodigal's father had long since forgiven his son. He knew all about how "lost" this lad was. Yet his thoughts were not on these familiar facts. Rather, they were on the day when all would be made right between him and his son.

A while ago, my wife and I began to leave our two sons alone at home for short periods of time with the older son in charge. He had reached the age where he could react responsibly enough to most of the expected crises in life. It allowed my wife and me a quieter shopping trip and gave the children a chance to put their feet upon furniture without the eyes bulging out of an over-zealous parent.

Lately, however, we've noticed a pattern that threatens to put an end to these occasions. Every time we go out, there are tell-tale signs of pilfering from the various containers of snack foods. Kathy and I encourage the boys to eat healthy, so we regulate their intake of junk food. In other words, we've put the kibosh on corn chips while we're not in the house.

We've known about the problem for some time, but we felt inwardly led to keep silent on the subject. One day after family devotions, the oldest son looked sheepish and pale. Immediately, my nurse-wife assumed he was sick. Well, there was a sickness, but it was not physical.

"Dad," he said, sheepishly, "I need you to know something."

"What is it, son?"

"I know it's wrong and all. Dad, I mean . . . will you forgive me?" He could not look up at me. Shock waves went through my psyche. Had he ax-murdered the neighbor's knotty-pine tree? What was he so tongue-tied and repentant about? I dug deeper.

"Forgive you for what?"

"Well, for being bad!" This begs the question, of course.

"What 'bad' thing did you do?"

"We sorta . . . I mean when you go out . . . I mean we did some stuff, you know?"

"You've been stealing snacks, haven't you?"

"You knew? You didn't say anything!"

"I wanted you to tell me. And I am so glad you did." Tears started to come to his eyes. They were already filling mine.

"It means something else, son," I added.

"What, Dad?"

"It means I can trust you. Anyone who can confess this problem on his own is old enough to have responsibilities." He heaved a sigh of relief as we held each other.

The key is to forgive as soon as possible after the offense is discovered. This gives the father a chance to be completely in control of the problem.

The father's role is to bring in love

The father in the prodigal parable could have reacted in a number of ways to his son's prepared speech. But what came out of Dad's mouth first is a lesson to be grabbed hold of.

"Father," the son said, "I have sinned against heaven and against you. I am no longer worthy to be called your son" (verse 21). As far as apologies go, this one was definitely designed to tug at the heartstrings. He called for pathos on behalf of his father.

How could the father have reacted? He could have said, "I'll show you to the servant's quarters." Or "Get out of my sight, you ingrate." He could have responded, "It's OK. You're still my son. I'll even help you set up a schedule to repay the money." Or "I forgive you. Don't let it happen again."

As much as some of these reactions seem entirely appropriate, this dad did not employ any of them. And instead of letting his boy take charge of this situation, he grabbed the emotional reins himself. He called for his servants and commanded them to dress his son in a fine robe and prepare a feast.

"This [son of mine] was dead and is alive again," he said (verse 24). Now, the past was dead. The poorly chosen path reconverged with the correct one, and all could now be rewritten.

This father's reaction goes against most of today's secular teaching. American poet Robert Frost condenses the predominant feeling of this world concerning the decisions we make (whether good or bad), in his poem "The Road Not Taken."

> I shall be telling this with a sigh,
> Somewhere ages and ages hence:
> Two roads diverged in a wood, and I—
> I took the one less travelled by,
> And that has made all the difference.

Frost took the nonconformist path at one point in his life, and whether right or wrong, it was his choice and it could not be unmade. But this is not the prevailing feeling displayed by the father of the prodigal. His son took a divergent road from what was accepted behavior. Unlike Frost, whom we can assume enjoyed the difference his radical road made for him, the son here did not enjoy his turn in the road of life. He despised the awful decision he had made.

The father was completely accurate in his pronouncement. His son's future died when he chose the sinful choice that led to separation from his father. Forgiveness was able to bring that relationship back to life and endue it with power to continue on.

The pouring out of a father's love, forgiveness and a sense of belonging are the essential ingredients in reconciliation. The transgressor has no reasonable hope that he will be accepted as he was before. Only the parent can provide the proof that there no longer exists an outstanding debt.

Love puts more emotion and effort into repairing the breach than it does in punishing the broken law. That is the Father's message from the Cross of Calvary. It is the message of grace.

Accepting the sinner

My mother gave me a grand picture of this kind of love several years ago. During my sophomore year of college, I volunteered to go on a summer missions program. The destination, as is obvious from the beginning of this chapter, was West Africa. Mom helped me raise my support, which was severely short up until the last moment when my grandmother provided the needed funds. I kissed Mom goodbye and set off to drive across the continent, from British Columbia to New York City. There I boarded a plane and flew to Africa.

Upon my return, I found to my dismay that my mother had moved. I vaguely remembered her telling me that it was possible she would be living back in our old hometown by the time I returned—so I drove the extra 70 miles there. I telephoned several family friends and finally found where she was living. When Mom opened the door, she at first said nothing. Then she began to sob. I had never seen her cry like that before. It made me feel honored. It gave me an air of the world traveler who was now safe with those who loved and accepted him.

Every child desires knowing these same heartfelt tears when he returns from his sin. Sin can take us much further away than Africa. It can bring a whole world between two people. When we give forgiveness as a gift, the sealing bow on this present is the celebration of love and joy.

History provides us with an ample picture of the value to be discovered in a love rejoined. On the night before Thomas Jefferson was to be inaugurated as president, he decided that it would be appropriate to regain the friendship of his old companion John Adams, whom he had just defeated in a bitterly fought election. He went to him, but before he could speak, Adams bellowed: "You have turned me out." The two never spoke again for 11 long years.

Then a friend of both these men, a medical doctor, was visiting the elderly Adams in his Boston home. At one point, Adams burst into tears and cried over the lost friendship. "I always loved that man," he said. "Will you tell him for me?" The message was quickly conveyed, and the two began a friendship again that they desperately needed. Their letters and conversations during those last years have become legend. They exchanged their ideas on life, liberty and the pursuit of happiness.

A rift need not be a road that diverges forever. Yet only in forgiveness is there a possibility of enough of God's love being released to raise a dead relationship back to life again.

If I could rewrite Frost's epic poem, I would say,

> I may be saying with a grin
> Sometime when memories are my store:
> Two roads diverged in a wood,
> I entered in
> And sought the lost one, who was my kin.
> And now those roads diverge no more.
> Forgiveness has now replaced the sin!

Dear President Kennedy:
This is my first letter I am writing on my new typewriter. I got the typewriter for my birthday and I wanted to send the first letter to you.
Please excuse any mistakes in this letter because the typewriter because the typewriter doesn't type so good yet.
Love
Barbara S. (age 11)
—(quoted by Bill Adler)

Chapter 10

Taking Children Beyond Self-Esteem

here is now an 11th Commandment: "Thou shalt not feel guilty." Guilt has been classified as the new demon of society's ills. Many psychiatrists and psychologists are trying to eliminate guilt so that they can eliminate the emotional traumas people face. Even one of the fad sermon ideas of recent times suggests that people will feel better about themselves if they eliminate the causes of their guilt.

Some of the same individuals promoting this teaching still discuss sin and forgiveness. But sin is no longer man's biggest problem—guilt and codependent attitudes are the "big two."

Don't misunderstand me. I can accept the existence of false guilt and codependent tendencies. What I cannot do is to give them premier billing in the show of life. And these concepts, real as they may be, have undermined the central concept of sin in some Christian counseling.

People want excuses for why they feel bad. Without overstating the case, let me list some of the generic ones: "He has a chemical imbalance." "She is under a lot of stress." "They have had poor scriptural teaching. If they could only get into a good church with a solid program." "She was abused and cannot grow up." "He just needs to believe in himself. If only his parents hadn't given him such a poor self-image." "She needs to speak the truth to herself and not believe the lies of the devil."

Again, do not misunderstand me. The above list may well be an accurate assessment of some of the struggles an individual faces in our world. But they are not now, and never have been, acceptable excuses for doing what is wrong.

Let me explain what I mean using the final excuse I mentioned. I have counseled individuals who were told that if they believed the devil's lies, they would have problems. I did not disagree with the statement. But I would ask them, "Did you ever confess this 'believing the lies of the devil' as a sin?" They would often look shocked.

Rejecting the truth for a lie is a sin. Yet we are told to view as victims those who believe the devil's lies. If they are victims, then they were victimized willingly.

What we've done is confused the word "excuse" with the word "reason." There are many contributing *reasons* to explain why we do wrong. Certainly, these may have to do with how we see ourselves, what we believe and how much tension exists in our lives. But it takes a quantum leap to allow reasons to become *excuses*. Excuses are the grounds upon which a guilty man may be declared free from punishment and guilt.

A recent example from a Montana courtroom points out the difference between these words. A college student entered the dormitory room of two other students and shot them dead. He fled the scene but was picked up by the police a few days later. The trial proceeded quickly due to the fact that all the evidence was extremely obvious. In his summation the defense attorney tried to convince the jury that his client should be declared innocent on the grounds of temporary insanity. He said that his client believed the two students had damaged his truck—his pride and joy! He lost his sanity for a moment and shot them.

Think about the reasoning of the attorney. First, he indicated that it was not normal for one person to kill another person for touching his truck. Second, that kind of reaction suggests a certain level of insanity. Third, since insanity has become an excuse for being lenient, his client should be declared innocent. The jury rejected this logic and threw the young man in jail. But this type of defense has succeeded elsewhere.

If we were to be biblically honest, *all* acts of sin

are the result of temporary insanity. What right-thinking human being would think of offending a God who is always watching and who holds his life in the space between his thumb and first finger? Insanity is still not an excuse for anything, though, especially not in the court of heaven.

Over his years of teaching golf, Chuck Cook has collected excuses for failure from professional golfers. Here are some of the more eloquent examples:

> "I didn't have time to warm up."
> "Why'd he turn the mower off just when I got over the ball?"
> "The fairway was too perfect to spot-aim."
> "The air's getting heavier."
> "The sun glared off the putter head."
> "I hit too many balls and left my game on the driving range."
> "I hurt my back this morning while I was brushing my teeth."
> (Quoted by Nick Seitz in *Golf Digest*, March 1991)

Golfer Greg Norman once claimed to have been distracted by a worm that popped out of the ground while he was on his downswing. Supposedly, this was the excuse he used to explain a nasty hook inserted into his fine round of golf. As an avid golfer myself, I have not been above using the occasional excuse every hole or so. But two things always bother me: No one ever believes me, and I never believe myself.

Poor self-esteem

In my counseling sessions, people have often excused their sin by blaming it on poor self-esteem. I have heard this approach both to explain why a spouse left when he should have stayed and why a spouse stayed when she should have left. Two separate books on my shelf suggest that I will do irreparable harm to my children if I allow them to grow up with a poor self-image. I find that hard to believe and even harder to accept when I observe how Father-God treats His children in the Bible.

The other day my wife reached her exasperation point while dealing with one of our sons. The point of contention had something to do with not turning off water faucets in the bathroom for the "one millionth time." The son in question said something sarcastic and earned an all-expense-paid trip to his bedroom. Kathy looked at me with utter hopelessness and exclaimed, "What is wrong with that kid?"

I answered, "He's a dirty, rotten sinner; the son of dirty, rotten sinners; and he lives in a dirty, rotten sinful world, where nothing good happens without God's direct intervention." I wasn't sure that was what she was after, and she asked me to repeat what I had said. So I expanded on my theory.

"He's just as bad as any other human being. There may be reasons for this, but they're minor compared to the fact that he's addicted to self—as are all people."

We talked for a while about this, and the conclusion we came up with was to throw out our efforts at trying to rehabilitate his "poor, submerged self-image." Actually, his self-image was right on the surface, alive and well and living in a messy bedroom down the hall. That was the same day I began to study God's Word, looking for His view of self-image. As a result of my investigation, I came to this conclusion: God says nothing about our self-image!

Not only that, but God does nothing to improve how we see ourselves. His approach is much different. He literally ignores how we view ourselves and, instead, pours out a constant stream of forgiveness and unconditional love. This stream flows from many tributaries, such as grace, mercy, acceptance, peace, tranquility and instruction.

These practices can be transferred to human fathers as long as we see *our children* the same way as God sees *us*—lost, due to sin's effects, and in need of much grace and undying love. And if we apply God's love and grace to our kids' lives, we can begin to see some remarkable results.

When the child fails life

My second-grade son waved a school paper in my face as I tried to read the newspaper. As I took it from him, it became obvious that I was holding a trophy in my hand, for I could see the victory lines etched in his smiling face. Here was a boy who had excelled above his peers to earn the award given to those who get all their math questions correct on a chapter exam. I knew he had labored long in studying for this test. He was proud, and I was genuinely proud—both for the result and the effort. He left me and showed his mother, who poured out similar accolades on him.

Then he went downstairs to do a character change.

Moments later we heard a fight beginning between our two sons. The now-famous math victor had left us holding the "A" paper and had gone to show it to his brother. He proceeded to tell his brother that they were going to play a game together. His brother refused, and a fight broke out.

What was curious to me is how a young boy can get an "A" in math and turn around and get an "F" in family relations. If there is an answer to this, it might be found in the first encounter between Father-God and Cain, the first son ever to give his mother a pain in the back.

Genesis 4:2–5 presents a scene that points out why kids act so self-oriented.

> Now Abel kept flocks, and Cain worked the soil. In the course of time Cain brought some of the fruits of the soil as an offering to the LORD. But Abel brought fat portions from some of the firstborn of his flock. The LORD looked with favor on Abel and his offering, but on Cain and his offering he did not look with favor. So Cain was very angry, and his face was downcast.

Abel was vice president of the new "All-World Family Survival Corporation." He was in charge of livestock. Cain was the other vice-president, and he was in charge of grain production. As commodities merchants, they took great pride and put great effort into their work. They were cognizant that God was the Supplier of their livelihood, and they acknowledged Him with offerings. So far, so good. They both get an "A" for intention.

Abel gave the firstfruits of his flock. He sacrificed the fattest of the firstborn and offered them to God. Cain gave some grain to God, but He did not accept Cain's offering. Some commentators have suggested that God had already instituted a system of blood sacrifices even at this early point in time. They reason that Cain's offering was rejected because it was only grain and not a blood sacrifice. But there are problems with this view. First, there is no evidence that God told them to offer up meat and not grain. Second, it seems unfair to allow Abel to give the fruit of his labor and not let Cain do the same thing.

There is a much simpler explanation. The wording of the original language for verse 3 suggests that Cain brought some leftover grain that he didn't need. In contrast, Abel gave the fattest of the firstborn as an offering. Cain's actions seem to be an act of religion. Abel's offering is laced with love and filial obedience. God accepted Abel because his heart condition was right; He rejected Cain because his heart was not right.

Perhaps today's "positive parent" would suggest

that the proper thing to do would have been to praise both children equally, rewarding them for their efforts. Positive parents don't play favorites. Positive parents build good self-esteem; they don't over-emphasize failure. They don't gloss over failure, but they do not dwell on it. At best, the correction should be mild. They would show the child how to offer a better offering—while still praising him for his good intentions.

But God does not follow this route. He expresses His displeasure at Cain, which injures his sense of self-worth. As a result, he goes into a hyper-pout. Pity is usually a wretched marriage of anger and rejection. Verse 6 shows this clearly: "Then the LORD said to Cain, 'Why are you angry? Why is your face downcast?' "

God confronts His son for allowing his feelings to be hurt. Today, Father-God would be criticized for these parental actions. But the Heavenly Father is not finished. Verse 7 continues,

> If you do what is right, will you not be accepted? But if you do not do what is right, sin is crouching at your door; it desires to have you, but you must master it.

This is a good passage for the father who wants to treat his kids the way Father-God treats His children. Love is always unconditional. But acceptance is not. God cannot accept what Cain is doing and continuing to do. It offends God, and His overriding concern is to get Cain's eyes off himself and onto the peril his soul is in. Cain, however, did not listen and quickly became the world's first murderer.

After this crime, Cain is unacceptable to God. Did God make a mistake? No. For children to grow up with a reasonable sense of propriety, they must be hit with the realities of what their own sinfulness has done. Their actions must be seen as failures, even though our love remains constant. But how can we achieve that balance?

Once again, the words of God give us the answer: "If you do what is right, will you not be accepted?" This statement offers a delicious and exciting promise of hope. It is the same kind of promise expressed in John 3:16, "whoever believes in him shall not perish but have eternal life." God is telling us that we can hope in His promise to change our relationship with Him only when we act in accordance with what He wants. This in no way implies that God is conditional with His love. But there can never be complete relationship rightness when we have not made things right.

"I won—or did I?"

One of my children has the habit of stubbornly refusing to go places with us. It's not that he dislikes our company; it's just his way of expressing his independence from us. Nor does he resort often to stubbornness. Yet the few times a year he goes through the "I-am-staying-in-this-car-and-Hulk-Hogan-can't-move-me" routine, I see red and threaten him with major bodily harm.

I never knew that anyone who weighs less than my golf-clubs could be so difficult to move just 30 feet. I have dragged, pushed, carried, bounced (don't ask) and once resorted to transporting him in an empty laundry basket.

Then one day I gave up the effort. It happened at a combined school track meet/picnic. Kathy made all of this kid's favorite foods. All his friends were going to be there. But somewhere from outer space, a hyperkinetic message reached him. It said, "It's not cool to go to school under your parents' rule, fool!" I can only guess about this transcosmic idea, for we were never able to figure out why he wouldn't get out of the car.

So I decided to leave him there. We were within sight of the car at all times, so we could not be accused of abandonment. Literally dozens of his friends came over to ask us where he was. We enigmatically pointed to the car each time. The stream of well-wishers and pout-breakers was seemingly endless. Yet he never emerged. He missed lunch. He missed games. He missed awards. He missed a lot of fun.

But when we returned to the car, he was wearing the faintest of smirks that suggested he had won. He was not aware of what he had actually lost. His mother tried to tell him, but there was a wad of spiritual cotton balls in his ears. He had got his way over us, and it was worth any price to do it.

So I raised the stakes. For the next two days, I had nothing to do with him. There were no hugs, stories, kisses, wrestling matches where Dad loses or tossing of footballs. There were no question-answer matches or reflective moments for his mental scrapbook.

Finally, after two days he came to me crying, "You don't love me anymore." I asked him why he felt that way, and he said that I wasn't acting like a dad any more. So I told him the rules: "You let me be in charge of this part of your life, and we'll do all the other stuff together."

He was silent to this pronouncement. He left me with both of us feeling as if he was the most forlorn offspring in the known world. As much as I wanted to run after him and gather him up in my arms, I could not do it. He had drawn a line in the sand, and as long as he would not acquiesce to my right to lead his life, he would have to know that it would affect our relationship.

I thought it would be a long time before he came back to talk with me. But five minutes later, he reappeared at the entrance to the living room.

"Dad, I'm sorry I've been bad. Will you forgive me?" He cried as he came over to me. We hugged and stroked one another's hair for a long time.

He has cut down on the amount of times that he acts in this self-centered way. But when he does, I am ready to show my displeasure and cut off some of the closeness.

I have also explained to my son how his selfishness can lead to other sins that have the power to hold him in bondage. I have been teaching him to confess his sin early and then renounce it in order to pull the rug out from under the devil's plans.

When a child gets an "F" in life, we as fathers must let him know in no uncertain terms that we are displeased—even though we will do the best thing for him in love. Love and acceptance are complicated, emotional concepts that are not easy to balance. God didn't want to destroy Cain's life— He wanted to destroy his overpowering sin. In our parenting we must not let sin go unchallenged. It does not benefit a child to accept him when his actions are sinfully unacceptable.

God in Heaven never accepted His children under such conditions.

When life fails the child

Most of the people who come to me for counseling, who think they have a poor self-image, refuse to point back to their own failures. They remember being abused, or neglected, or unloved, or unacceptable to their parents. They remember ridicule and jokes about how they looked. They remember heartaches and tragedies, some of them reaching epic proportions. But many of them find it hard to acknowledge their sinful actions or their sinful reactions to the ordeals they faced.

Anyone reading the previous section might say, "I can see how it is wrong to build up self-esteem in an erring child, but isn't it right to strengthen the self-image of someone who has been destroyed by abuse and rejection?"

This is a critical point. Some people may assume that the ignominious treatment received by these people in earlier years sets up a pattern of thinking that destroys their internal self-worth in later years—"If people rejected me, then I must not be worth accepting." The therapy then for this soul disease is to rebuild the wounded sense of self-worth. A Christian who practices this might point to God's dying on the Cross as a proof of our worth. After all, would God send His Son if we were not worth everything to Him? Simply put, people with poor self-images cannot function normally in life because they have been conditioned to think too little of themselves.

But here's the rub: The proposed solution to this dilemma does not recognize poor self-esteem as the common condition of fallen man, and every injustice only strengthens the feeling. The woman caught in adultery in John 8 shows us this principle.

> Jesus went to the Mount of Olives. At dawn he appeared again in the temple courts, where all the people gathered around him, and he sat down to teach them. The teachers of the law and the Pharisees brought in a woman caught in adultery. They made her stand before the group and said to Jesus, "Teacher, this woman was caught in the act of adultery. In the Law Moses commanded us to stone such women. Now what do you say?" They were using this question as a trap, in order to have a basis for accusing him.
>
> But Jesus bent down and started to write on the ground with his finger. When they kept

> on questioning him, he straightened up and said to them, "If any one of you is without sin, let him be the first to throw a stone at her." Again he stooped down and wrote on the ground.
>
> At this, those who heard began to go away one at a time, the older ones first, until only Jesus was left, with the woman still standing there. Jesus straightened up and asked her, "Woman, where are they? Has no one condemned you?"
>
> "No one, sir," she said.
>
> "Then neither do I condemn you," Jesus declared. "Go now and leave your life of sin." (verses 1-11)

This is a woman who, according to verse 3, was caught in the act of adultery. This was not an easy thing to do for her accusers, because most people do not commit adultery in places where they are likely to be seen or caught. Some Bible teachers have suggested that this woman was set up so that the Pharisees could have a perfect specimen with which to accuse Jesus. Whether she was set up or not, the Pharisees seized the opportunity to use her to discredit Jesus.

If He publicly condemned her, Jesus would make a mockery of the grace and forgiveness of God He was preaching. If He exonerated her, He would put Himself in opposition to the Law of Moses. I'm glad I didn't have this kind of question on my final theology exam!

There are many loose ends to this story. For instance, where was the man who was with the woman? What did Jesus write on the ground? What would Jesus have answered them? Why did He write twice on the ground? Why did the men leave? Others will have to fill in these cerebral blanks. But somehow, Jesus' digital dust-writing drew a bead on their consciences, pricking their self-esteem. As they left one by one, the woman must have been filled with a mixture of relief and bewilderment. The scene was not over, though.

Hockey sticks hurt!

I have been in this position several times in my growing up years. One day, when my friends and I were playing hockey on the road in front of our house, my brother's stick came up during a goal-mouth tussle, and it caught me square in the mouth. Blood began to pour out of the now-swelling upper lip. I swore at him all the way into the house as he profusely apologized.

I entered the basement door and let go a four-letter word that I had never used before. My father was standing right there as I opened the door. He had been fixing something in the basement. When he saw my bleeding lip, he sent me upstairs to clean it up. Then he spoke to my brother.

Several minutes later, Dave came in and apologized again. This time I accepted his apology. I felt that because Dad had sent him in, I was off the hook for the swear word. I began to feel like I was the injured party and that I had a right to say that word.

Dad came into the bathroom next and asked how my lip was. I told him it hurt, and he suggested I put some ice on it. I was about to leave when he grabbed my shoulder roughly. "Hold it, young man," he said. "We're not finished. Do you mind repeating what you said?"

"No, sir," I responded with my head down. If I had a tail, it would have gone between my legs.

"If I ever, *ever* catch you saying that again, you will never forget what happens next."

Needless to say, I never uttered that word again. I also was shocked into the reality of knowing that my dad held me completely responsible for my behavior, irrespective of what my brother had done to me.

Jesus brings this point home to the woman caught in adultery. He asked her, "Woman, where are they? Has no one condemned you?" The condemnation He is referring to is not the same as a rebuke for her sin. He is speaking of a condemnation that results in the death penalty. He would not give her the death penalty, which is not to say she didn't deserve it.

According to Jewish law, she could have been stoned for her sin. But in His declaration, "neither do I condemn you," Jesus offered healing for the shame and rejection she must have felt. People who have been hurt by life's injustices need to be healed by Jesus. But His healing is not equivalent to improving their self-images.

Jesus then says, "Go now and leave your life of sin." He does not whitewash her past, nor is this an attempt to rescue her from a poor self-image. It is an act of unconditional love and forgiveness, without accepting the crime committed.

In Mark 2:1–12, Jesus heals a paralytic who was let down through a roof by his friends. Before He healed him, though, Jesus dealt with his spiritual condition. He said, "Son, your sins are forgiven" (verse 5). I've often wondered why He used the word "son." No matter how young this man was, Jesus was not that old; He probably was around 30 at this point in His ministry. I've come to the conclusion that Jesus is representing the Father. He wants to deal with the man's sin before healing him. He does this to accomplish two things: First, He wants to show the Pharisees that He has authority to forgive sins. Second, He desires to point out that He heals as an act of mercy—not because the man is worth being healed.

God wants to heal the brokenness of our children's past, and we can pray for the rejections they face. At age 26, I was prayed for and received healing from awful memories of rejection that I experienced as a child. But the one who prayed for me gave me this caution. The competitive spirit, the lying and the selfish, unloving attitude I constantly expressed toward other people could not be excused by those hurts I had endured. I had to confess my sin, renounce it and turn away from it before my healing from the past would be complete.

I teach my kids this principle. As their father I want to heal all the vagaries and mishaps in their lives. But even more than that, I want to see them delivered from the sin that locks them in selfishness and self-protecting behavior.

Every night when my kids bed down, I tell them the same thing: "God loves you always. I love you. So does your mother. Forgive those who hurt you. But ask God to forgive you for anything wrong you have done."

When life fails the child, there is the healing grace of God. But when the child fails life, no inner healing can eradicate the besetting sin. Only repentance can heal sin. A good father will show his children how to repent!

Poor self-esteem is a four-letter word

The rest of my drama class was hard at work perfecting their writing assignments. I had already completed my script. It was easy: I borrowed a short story from Kurt Vonnegut Jr., added a few lines, took out the narrative and put in a few minor characters to spice up the script. Then I called it "An *Adaptation* of Kurt Vonnegut Jr.'s 'Thomas Edison's Shaggy Dog,'" and signed my name to it. My creative effort at prolonged laziness pleased the teacher—she even gave me a high mark.

So I sat in class with nothing to do but pester the other kids. Some of them found out what I had done and accused me of plagiarism. Since I called my work an "adaptation," the teacher came to my defense. My classmates, most of whom were close friends, were royally ticked off at me. My gloating was a great contributing factor in their furor. Normally, my pride and self-importance didn't bother most of them. They had grown accustomed to my bragging about grades and accomplishments. They ignored the white lies with which I peppered the conversation. But this time they were really mad.

As they shied away from me, I moped. Even when they forgot about it all, I moped. When they went on to other things and wanted to include me, I told them to go away, for I was depressed. "Why do you want to hang around with a loser like me?" I queried them. They tried to build me up, but all they did was drive me deeper into gloom.

Inside I was enjoying every minute of it.

My brother, however, burst the balloons at my pity-party. This is what he said: "Ignore Mike. He gets depressed and down on himself about once a year. Ignore it and he'll stop."

So they ignored me, and my pity-party was over. All the invited guests had left. Dave had seen me go into the "seven woes of my life" just about every year of our growing up together. My parents refused to coddle me during my moments of moodiness.

My brother and sister chose to ignore me when I was in these throes of despair. My friends, who had rarely witnessed this abject cry for attention, took a while longer to notice the hoax I was trying to pull on them. This bothered me inside—for I fully expected them to give me the recognition and ego-stroking I desired.

When they began to ignore my histrionics, I really became depressed. Now I found that I could not turn it off and on as I wanted. Bitterness began to seep into my spirit as I viewed my poor, wretched life. The depression deepened, and I found myself sleeping longer and longer and eating less and less. Clinical signs of what some might call paranoia began to show up in my psyche.

As I look back at this far-distant time, I can see some of the contributing reasons for my lethargic funk. I had grown up with certain internal images about myself. Through various circumstances, I felt as if no one cared about me until I did something spectacular. I also was terribly afraid of being looked upon as a second-place finisher.

Other messages mingled with this internal imaging and produced a false image of my life. I believed that lie, and it left me with several decisions to make. And most of the ones I made were sinful. They resulted in more anguish, more pity, more depression, more suicidal thoughts and more bitterness.

I am not saying in this chapter that people do not have poor, misguided and even downright evil self-images. They do. But I am not ready to admit that our self-images are the primary source of the feelings we have about ourselves.

Don Matzat, in his book *Christ Esteem*, brings out a neglected point about the early life of Adam, the first man. He states,

There is good evidence to suggest that Adam

was not self-conscious prior to his falling into sin. While the Bible does not specifically make that statement, the content of the Genesis account—together with the call of the Gospel away from "self" and into Jesus—leads to that conclusion.

Adam did not think about himself in the Garden of Eden. What he was most aware of was the job at hand, the woman at his side, the animals as companions and the God who fashioned it all. It was paradise because *self* was not there. As soon as Adam sinned, though, he became totally aware of himself, resulting in his fig-leaf cover-up. God's question to Adam after his sin was this: "Who told you that you were naked?" (Genesis 3:11).

It is sin that causes us to be completely self-absorbed. In our sinfulness we react to the messages around us with a twisted, truncated action that leads these messages to form a weird self-image. Then we come to the results of that ill-formed self-image.

We always have a choice whether or not to believe a message. And we can always choose how we will act according to that message. In helping a child who has a wrong image of himself, there must always be two parts to the ministry.

First, it is good to bring in the truth. Speak the loving truth without embellishment. As fathers, we have a tendency to tell our children—more than they need to hear—how wonderful they are. None of us are wonderful. We are loved and cared for—

but we fall at least two heavens short of wonderful. Only God is good. Only God is wonderful.

But after the truth-telling comes the conviction of sins committed. As the pastor who prayed for my inner healing reminded me, "Poor self-image is not an excuse to sin. Poor self-image is the result of sinful reactions. Renounce your sin and be forgiven." We must make it clear to our children that they cannot act any way they want just because they feel rejected, hurt or angry. The reason there has been a recent backwash of books blasting self-image teaching is that this teaching seems to be granting an excuse for past sin through the discovery of internal past images. Internal images began with Adam—and he didn't have anyone around to reject him or to abuse him. Adam felt guilty because he was guilty!

Of course, some people feel guilt because of someone else's actions. Codependents feel guilt with someone else. Sexual abuse victims feel guilty because of the sin of another. But how a person reacts, even after being abused, still has to be accounted for.

Jezebel was out to get him

You have to empathize with Elijah for the emotional firestorm that was going on within him as he fell exhausted on Mount Horeb. In First Kings 19 we witness an extraordinary event in the history of the Bible and our world. Elijah had just killed the prophets of Baal at the battle of the gods. King Ahab sped home to tell his wife Jezebel the outcome of the event. Jezebel, angered at the news, sent a message to Elijah swearing to do him in. Amazingly (after all, Elijah had just seen God achieve a mighty victory), Elijah fears for his life and scoots out of town.

He heads out into the desert below Beersheba and finally comes to a broom tree where he sits down to rest. The Lord then feeds him two square meals and sends him on his way again, to Mount Horeb, which Scripture calls "the mountain of God" (verse 8).

At the mountain, God speaks to Elijah, who is still reveling in self-pity. But that was about to change, for the Lord was going to take charge of the situation.

> The LORD said, "Go out and stand on the mountain in the presence of the LORD, for the LORD is about to pass by."
>
> Then a great and powerful wind tore the mountains apart and shattered the rocks before the LORD, but the LORD was not in the wind. After the wind there was an earthquake, but the LORD was not in the earthquake. After the earthquake came a fire, but the LORD was not in the fire. And after the fire came a gentle whisper. When Elijah heard it, he pulled his cloak over his face and went out and stood at the mouth of the cave.
>
> Then a voice said to him, "What are you doing here, Elijah?"
>
> He replied, "I have been very zealous for the

LORD God Almighty. The Israelites have rejected your covenant, broken down your altars, and put your prophets to death with the sword. I am the only one left, and now they are trying to kill me too."

The LORD said to him, "Go back the way you came, and go to the Desert of Damascus. When you get there, anoint Hazael king over Aram . . . Jehu son of Nimshi king over Israel, and anoint Elisha . . . to succeed you as prophet. Jehu will put to death any who escape the sword of Hazael, and Elisha will put to death any who escape the sword of Jehu. Yet I reserve seven thousand in Israel—all whose knees have not bowed down to Baal and all whose mouths have not kissed him." (verses 11–18)

Look what God did for Elijah. He fed him twice, called him, spoke to him, revealed His presence in a quiet way and let him vent his feelings of self-pity and bitterness. God brought comfort and strength. He listened with a sympathetic ear. But God also saw that His servant was stuck in his poor self-image. Elijah was developing a "loner" complex, believing that he stood alone against all the forces of evil.

God clears that falsehood up in a hurry: "I reserve seven thousand . . . whose knees are not bowed down to Baal and whose mouths have not kissed him." God also appoints some men to be directly involved in the ministry of turning Israel's hearts toward Him. Hazael will be in charge of military shock troops. Jehu will replace evil King Ahab. And Elisha will be Elijah's successor. Elijah seems satisfied with God's words.

What can we do for our children when their lives start to crumble around them? We need to care for their immediate needs first. Then we need to ask them to explain the situation as they see it. When we have discovered their feelings on the matter, we need to carefully cut out the errors and half-truths and splice in the truth where it is appropriate. When this is finished, offer to give them whatever assistance you can in the battle against a false understanding of how their lives are proceeding. Then it will be necessary for them to confront their self-pity. In essence, this is what God did for Elijah. Elijah needed to see that he was feeling unduly sorry for himself.

We could spell poor self-image in just four letters: P-I-T-Y. And if self-pity is not brought into check, it will lengthen to 10 letters: B-I-T-T-E-R-N-E-S-S. In Acts 8:20 Peter warns Simon the Sorcerer of this. When Simon wanted to buy the ability to bestow the Holy Spirit on people, Peter told him, "May your money perish with you, because you thought you could buy the gift of God with money!" Simon was a man whose life had been bent toward impressing others. Perhaps he had grown up neglected and rejected. Perhaps his life was a garble of mixed messages to which he constantly responded by trying to impress others. Peter doesn't deal with that at all. First, he clarifies the truth for Simon. *God's gifts are free gifts.* This "truth therapy" hurts, but it becomes the sword of the Spirit for scalpeling away the lies of the enemy.

But Peter does not excuse Simon either. In verses 22–23 he says, "Repent of this wickedness and pray to the Lord. Perhaps he will forgive you for having such a thought in your heart. For I see that you are full of bitterness and captive to sin."

Peter did not allow error to go unchecked into bitterness. Bitterness is the most loathsome form of depression, for it rarely responds to any kind of treatment and always spreads to other people.

The key to dealing with our children in this area is to do what Father-God often does: challenge the lies and confront the sins. But there is another factor in all of this, and it lies in the circle of understanding that most of us call our self-worth.

Going beyond self-worth

A fascinating word study in the Bible is the concept of worth. In my computer concordance, there are many verses using the word "worth." As I looked through it recently, I was trying to find portions that spoke of man's worth to God. I eliminated all the verses that had to do with the worth of a cow, or a vineyard, or a king. Once I had deleted the "relative worth" verses, there weren't many left—two to be exact, after accounting for duplicate verses in the Gospels.

Here they are: "So don't be afraid; you are worth more than many sparrows" (Matthew 10:31). "In-

stead, it should be that of your inner self, the un-
fading beauty of a gentle and quiet spirit, which is
of great worth in God's sight" (1 Peter 3:4).

Though these verses are short, they are descrip-
tive of our intrinsic worth as human beings. The
first one occurs in the middle of a chapter where
Jesus is teaching about God's willingness to supply
our daily needs. The verse before this one reminds
us that two sparrows are sold for a penny. Therefore, we can conclude that we at least are worth a
few bucks! Taken at face value, this is not very
reassuring. However, we are assured of God's
loving-kindness in this verse, for He promises to
care for the daily needs of His children.

The second verse is speaking to wives in Christ
whose husbands are not believers. Peter exhorts
them to be beautiful inside, winning their husbands over with a gentle and quiet spirit, which
God values highly. It is not a statement of intrinsic
worth or created worth. It is a value judgment on
one particular set of righteous deeds.

Neither of these verses, then, affirms the value of
man. Some people have said that our worth is implied. Because we are made in the image of God,
we must be of great worth to Him. Yet in many
places in God's Word we are told that He is the pot-
ter and we are the clay; He can do as He pleases
with us. And Romans 3:12 says, "All have turned
away,/ they have together become worthless." We
find similar messages in Second Kings 17:15 and
Isaiah 40:17.

Still another person has written, "We were of

such value to God that God sent His Son Jesus to die for us." To be gentle with the person who wrote this, I can only say that this teaching is poor doctrine. The only reason God decided to send Jesus to the Cross was His unconditional love—not our worth. If we had intrinsic worth before the Cross, Jesus would be obligated to die for us. But in our sin, we abrogated all of our worth. As sinners saved by grace, we have Jesus' worth imputed to us. We give Jesus our worthlessness, and He gives us His worth and righteousness in exchange.

Why should God love us? I have no idea! That is what makes grace amazing!

"I'll love you forever"

My daughter carries with her an old, tattered blanket that she refers to as her "night-night." We can no longer wash it, for it would immediately disintegrate when the first rinse cycle hit. So the blanket crumbles and decays and picks up layers of dirt, making it a good site for germ warfare tests. Joyous at finding a place unaffected by cleanliness, new organisms form there every day.

Meaghan loves that blanket implicitly. But lately, its appearance has offended even her. In the last few weeks, she has suggested we burn it. Her nicknames for it are no longer filled with affection. Its holes and grime are even causing her to stay away from it.

This is an example of conditional love. But Jesus came into our filth, which was a million times more torturous to Him than my daughter's blanket is to us, to show us unconditional love. He embraced our disease and touched our inner leprosy.

As a father, I want to pass the knowledge of God's love on to my children. I want to become for them what my Heavenly Father is for me—an unending lover. I believe this begins with imagining the worst thing my children could ever do to me. I have then made the follow-up decision to imagine myself continuing to love them no matter what. If you think that this is an act of nonsense, consider what God has done for us. In creating us, He certainly understood the possibility of what we could do to Him. Yet notwithstanding all those awful possibilities, He became our Father and fashioned for Himself a part of creation that would be the object of His unconditional love.

One of my son's favorite books is called *Love You Forever* by Robert Munsch. The story revolves around a mother whose nightly habit is to sneak quietly into the bedroom of her son while he is sleeping and sing a song to him. She does this when he is a toddler, when he is a school-aged boy and when he becomes a teenager. My favorite scene is when he moves away from home. The mother loads up a ladder and drives to her son's residence. She climbs up to his window and, while he is sleeping, sings him the same song. The story tenderly ends when the mother is too old to go and sing to her son. So he goes to her hospital room and holds her while singing the same song. This is the song:

I'll love you forever,
I'll like you for always,
As long as I'm living,
My baby you'll be.

As I've stated earlier, you cannot spoil children
by pouring out love and affection on them. You
cannot spoil your kids by making them objects of
your caring—something they do not seek. No child
became a whiny, mewling brat because his parents
caressed him with words of love and strokes of
healing closeness. The song above suggests that
only a "forever" love is adequate to overcome the
sin nature our children have inherited from us.

If we seek to give them a sense of worth, we may
find ourselves in conflict with the need to battle
self-destructive attitudes and actions. But a course
of action that does not tolerate selfishness, yet always pours out love, will bypass the question of
worth and wrap our children in a comforting
cocoon of God's covenant love.

The best thing you'll ever do!

What would God's last words to human fathers
be? John 17 is called the "High Priestly Prayer" of
Jesus. In these 26 verses Jesus represents us before
the Father, asking Him to protect us by the power
of His name. At the end of that prayer, I see a message to the Heavenly Father on behalf of us earthly
fathers:

Righteous Father, though the world does not

know you, I know you, and they know that
you have sent me. I have made you known to
them, and will continue to make you known
in order that the love you have for me may be
in them and that I myself may be in them.
(verses 25–26)

We see from Jesus' words that knowing the
Father is the exclusive right of God's children. This
is also my all-encompassing desire: to know the
Father and, in that knowledge, rearrange my life so
that I am like Him—even if that means I break
with current fads in fathering. The world does not
know the Father, but I can know Him intimately
because of His Son Jesus who lives in me by faith.

In this book I have explored a bare minimum of
anecdotes and passages relating to Father-God. But
even this elementary knowledge has the potential
to grind us to a halt in our earthly mistakes and set
us on a course to parental liberation. Jesus has
made the Father known, and that knowledge can
give us the picture of the perfect parent.

All we have looked at can be distilled into a
single proof word: LOVE. I don't mean "Love
Boat," feel-good love but the kind that God has—
never-ending, demonstrated, taught and discussed.
My prayer for human fathers is that each one will
place his fathering on the altar, asking God continually to fill him with His love.

Several days before my father died, I went into
his bedroom at his request. He lay there in the
emaciated shell of his once-robust body. Yet his

mind was as clear and concise as ever. I believe that even with the painkillers and confusion of that time, he instinctively knew that his death was imminent. We shared together a conversation that was to be our last.

"Michael," he said, "I want you to know something. It has taken me an entire life to realize that all of the things I really felt were important had nothing to offer me."

"Why, Dad?"

"Because they dealt only with what *I* wanted in life. All I ever wanted was to make myself happy. And it has cost me my life." Of course, he was referring to his cancer. His breathing was now so shallow that he had to stop for a moment to catch his breath. Then he continued.

"I want you to know this, son."

"What?"

"I love you. It's the best thing I'll ever do."

I cried then. I cry now. I will cry again when he holds me in his arms in heaven, and my Heavenly Father unites us.

Love your children, fathers. It's the best thing you'll ever do!